Advance Praise

FANTASTIC! André is a true inspiration and a polished public speaker. I had the privilege of hearing André speak at an association meeting a few months ago, and it was one of the best lectures I have heard to date. André draws from his personal experiences—including his battles with blindness and cancer—to inspire, motivate, and encourage you not to fear change or allow circumstances to deter you from achieving your goals. His story was captivating. In *The Curiosity of Change*, André drives home his message that, with curiosity and perseverance, you can achieve anything you put your mind to. I highly recommend André for your next speaking engagement.

James Reisig, General Manager, Union Club of the City of New York

Feedback about André's *The Curiosity of Change* presentation has been tremendous. He clearly was a hit with this group. Attendees praised both the content and the delivery—an all-too-rare combination.

Debbie Taylor, Meetings Industry Council of Colorado Chair, 2015

André spoke to my organization of more than 300 people, and he captivated and inspired a room full of individuals. At a time where we as an organization are managing change and increasing workloads, he touched everyone with *The Curiosity of Change* and how we should embrace our journey. People are still reflecting on his words, and he left a lasting positive impact on Denver Technology Services. Thank you, André!

Scott Cardenas, CIO, City of Denver, Colorado

André's presentation, *The Curiosity of Change*, was exceptional—engaging and inspiring. Periodically, I would look across the room and my entire team, without exception, was completely captivated. André sensed exactly the kind of message I was trying to share with my team, and he did so in a manner that ranged from heart-wrenching to humorous.

David Craig, General Manager, C Lazy U Ranch, Granby, Colorado

André is most certainly an inspiring leader with a compelling personal story of dealing with a transformational change that impacted every aspect of his life. As a speaker, his willingness to share his personal experiences and show his vulnerability built a strong platform of trust. Those aspects in and of themselves are reasons to engage André as a speaker or consultant. But even more impactful is his ability to inform, educate, and inspire individuals to excel as leaders and offer tools to guide them through that evolution. In person and in his remarkable new book, *The Curiosity of Change*, André tells it like it is. He provides a mix of empathy for the challenges leaders face and his straightforward challenge to be the best leader one can be. We will continue to engage André for future speaking opportunities and for coaching and executive management training.

Tami Door, President and CEO,
Downtown Denver Partnership, Denver, Colorado

The
Curiosity
of Change

The
Curiosity
of Change

How to Bring Light
to the Dark Side of Change

André van Hall

The Curiosity of Change: How to Bring Light to the Dark Side of Change
Published by Pelham Publishing Company
Denver, CO

Publisher's Cataloging-in-Publication data

Names: van Hall, F. André, author.
Title: The curiosity of change: how to bring light to the dark side of change / by André van Hall.
Description: First trade paperback original edition. | Denver [Colorado] : Pelham Publishing Company, 2019. Also being published as an ebook.
Identifiers: ISBN 978-0-578-40486-8
Subjects: LCSH: Business. | Leadership. | Mentoring. | Strategic planning. | Business communication.
BISAC: BUSINESS / Leadership.
Classification: LCC HF5549.5.M63 | DDC 658.409–dc22

QUANTITY PURCHASES: Schools, companies, professional groups, clubs, and other organizations may qualify for special terms when ordering quantities of this title. For information, email andre@andrevanhall.com.

This book is printed in the United States of America.

To Nancy, for guiding me through the darkness

Contents

Foreword

FOR FIFTEEN YEARS, I THOUGHT I KNEW ANDRÉ VAN Hall. We served on boards together and played racquetball together, and I truly enjoyed his company. I had gotten to really know the guy I admired and respected more than anyone else I know, when André suddenly lost his sight. I have never seen a person who has lost one of his primary senses handle such a devastating change with more courage, grace, and positive attitude.

His book *The Curiosity of Change* is a must-read for all of us, because we all experience change, whether it is Environmental, Purposeful, or Disruptive change. André discusses those three types of change in a thoughtful and practical way.

After losing his eyesight, André could have spent his days on the couch feeling sorry for himself. Instead, he is inspiring others with this remarkable book and with his lively speaking engagements. André challenges us to *assess* with an open mind rather than *judge* based on our past experiences. He challenges us to be curious, to get out there and start imagining, then to take action. You can't do these things from the couch!

When faced with change and its challenges, we each have options. I love the choices and options André has embraced and encourages you to think about. In his words, "Change is inevitable. Personal growth is optional." André van Hall has taken personal growth to a whole new level.

Scott Bemis
Director of Business and Community Partnerships
Plante Moran, a global company specializing in audit, tax,
consulting, and wealth management

Introduction

I GREW UP IN BUENOS AIRES, ARGENTINA. WE HAD A
ranch in Entre Rios, a province just northeast of the city, so I was
blessed with a dual life—the formality of the city and the casual
lifestyle of a truly rural environment.

I attended a British, all-boys school in Argentina where I was
the smallest in my class of sixteen. Being the smallest had huge
significance. We played rugby and soccer. I sucked at both, and
because of my size, I was relentlessly humiliated, brutally beaten,
and forced into fights for most of my years there. The more they
hazed me because I did not smoke or drink, the more obstinate I
became not to bend to their will.

I then did my compulsory military service by serving in the
Argentinean coast guard. This was during one of the darkest chap-
ters in Argentinean history, the Dirty War. Cuba had fallen to Castro,
and Che Guevara was agitating throughout Latin America. Chile and

Peru had already fallen to communism, and Argentina and Uruguay were well on their way. The ideological fight between capitalism and communism divided our country and precipitated some of the greatest human rights atrocities imaginable, on both sides.

My mother always wanted me to become a doctor or a lawyer, but during my tenure in the coast guard, as a waiter to the officers, I became attracted to the idea of a career in hospitality. My mother insisted that if I were to become a waiter, I must become the best. After she convinced me to research the best hotel schools, I chose a fine school in Lausanne, Switzerland, but they required me to gain some practical experience before admittance. The day I turned in my coast guard uniform, I left my war-torn country to seek my fortune in the hospitality industry by starting as a pot washer at the renowned Hotel Vier Jahreszeiten in Hamburg, Germany.

I went through an enormous culture shock, not only to learn German and immerse myself in that country's way of life but also to adapt to being at the very bottom of the totem pole. I was promoted to dishwasher, then I apprenticed throughout the kitchen, working in the saucier, entremetier, garde manger, poissonier, and pâtissier departments. I then moved to the front of the house in the dining room and front desk. You could say that this was already a lot of change. My general manager in the Hotel Vier Jahreszeiten, who had graduated from the Lausanne hotel school I had aspired to attend, took me under his wing, saying, "André, the future is in American hotel schools, where they teach more about business and less about service."

Then he told me that his colleague, the general manager at the Ritz in Paris, needed someone with my language skills, so the next day I found myself on a train, Paris-bound, to work at this other world-famous establishment as a telex operator.

A year later, I was admitted to the School of Hotel Administration at Cornell University, graduating in 1980. From there, I was whisked off to New York City to work at the monstrous Sheraton New York Hotel & Towers as director of quality and then at the St. Regis as executive assistant manager. Three years later, I was on my way to Miami to open two hotels as rooms executive and resident manager.

With a failed marriage behind me, I next moved to open a hotel in Washington, D.C., where I met my wife, Nancy, through a personal ad in *Washingtonian* magazine. I promptly moved to Burlington, Vermont, for my first general manager job at the Radisson Hotel. I was only thirty-three.

I subsequently moved to Atlanta to take the helm of the Hyatt Regency Hotel then, with two babies in tow, on to Louisville, Kentucky, to rescue the distressed Hyatt Regency there. Six years later, I moved to Denver, Colorado, to run the 1,200-room Adam's Mark Hotel. When it was put up for sale five years later, I accepted the job as CEO of the historic Denver Athletic Club, where I spent ten wonderful years.

Is that enough change for you? No? Good, because there is more. I lost my eyesight suddenly—first one eye, then the other. I lost my job. I received a diagnosis no one wants to hear—cancer. The changes kept on coming and after many years in hospitality, I became a professional speaker and author.

I think you would agree that I have seen significant change in my life. The changes were of all kinds: environmental (health issues, growing older, etc.), purposeful (choosing my career, decisions others made that affected my life, getting married, etc.), and finally, disruptive changes like getting divorced, losing my eyesight, and losing my job. In *The Curiosity of Change*, as I talk about changes I experienced, I am not by any means trying to "compete" with the changes that have happened in your life. This is not a "show me yours and I will show you mine" kind of story. My purpose is to explore change, regardless of how deep that change is. We are all together in the fact that we face change, constant change, brutal change. I hope to show you that by being curious, not only can you adapt to change but, ideally, stay ahead of it.

CHANGE AND YOU

You've experienced unwanted change and disruptive change. If you're like the rest of us, you've tried to avoid change and found that doesn't work. You've also initiated some changes on purpose because of what you wanted to accomplish or achieve. I know you. I *am* you. Each of us is confronted with change, all the time.

So what about you? You want to change your current situation, but you are plagued by thoughts that block your ability to bring the change about. Things beyond your control won't allow you to move forward. You are looking for the motivation to take the first step.

The purpose of this book is to help you, dear reader, stay a step ahead of change, to show you that *curiosity* is the answer to becoming a change agent. Because in today's world, incremental change is the price of entry into the race of life. We can no longer afford to stand still and pretend that, although other people might need to change, we like ourselves just the way we are. That can be one of our greatest blind spots.

Change comes in three variations: Environmental Change is distinctly different from Purposeful Change. Severe environmental change or severe purposeful change can lead to Disruptive Change:

- Environmental Change—the type that simply happens: you age, a cold winter kills your crop, you get a bad diagnosis
- Purposeful Change—the type you make happen on purpose, or someone else does and it affects you
- Disruptive Change—environmental or purposeful change with deep, deep consequences (good or bad) triggered by you or by someone else.

In this book, I want to show you how to embrace curiosity, disruption, and imagination. I want to teach you to see yourself as a change agent.

Here's the good news: becoming a change agent is not hard. You just need to look at things with a curious mind. Engage the people around you in a quest for curiosity. All around you, people are bringing change about. You no longer have a choice about whether or not you want to change!

My life has been disrupted by all three kinds of change, and those changes forced me to be curious. Most of the change has been intentional or purposeful, but some of it was environmental and certainly disruptive.

From hazings to military service, to adapting to four different cultures (Argentinean, German, French, and American), to moving thirteen times, to working with many different corporations and transitions from hotels to clubs, to experiencing a divorce then a new marriage and children, and going from healthy to sick—all these changes have offered me the opportunity to become more curious and to overcome my own psychological and mental blind spots.

This whole process has left me with valuable insights about change. I am able to see change as the cause of many of the adaptations, but not necessarily as the enemy of the status quo. I learned how to bring about purposeful change to achieve my vision. I learned how to overcome some of the most disruptive changes imaginable.

When I decided to become a speaker, I was certainly qualified to talk about service or management but, after realizing how change had affected my life—for better and for worse—I decided to help other people just like me see that change is not our enemy. Change will happen! You will make change happen! Our potential enemy is *how we react to the change.* The enemy is change that grabs us unaware because we stood rigidly and neglected to stay informed, or seek input, or ask for help from others, or challenge our current thinking.

Our blind spots are the enemy.

WHY CURIOSITY?

We keep hearing that change is accelerating, that it is inevitable, that we need to get with it or get left behind ... that being open to change is a matter of *attitude.*

But how do I wake up your attitude? What if you are afraid of change? You are tired of everything changing around you; you don't care to keep up. What could I possibly do to help you open your mind to change? Everything I thought about trying sounded preachy and possibly insurmountable for those of you who do not embrace or even enjoy change.

My family and friends woke me up. That is, they woke up my curiosity to help me transition into blindness—to learn to use a cane, to explore the availability of assistive devices such as screen-readers or talking watches, even to ride a tandem bicycle. I began to ride away from "Why me?" and pedal rapidly toward "Why not?" I began to understand that I needed to be more curious about alternative solutions and outcomes. That propelled me to apply my life-long passion for thinking outside of the box. I realized that, at least in one sense, nothing had changed—I was in charge of how the world perceived me.

After I saw a documentary on Albert Einstein, I realized the importance of curiosity, not only to adapt to change but also to get in front of change. When Einstein was asked about his intelligence, he replied, "I have no special talent. I am only passionately curious."

What an epiphany! We don't need to be smart—we need to be curious. And I do know how to wake up your curiosity. Just as family and friends awakened my curiosity, I know that *The Curiosity of Change* will be a catalyst to help you bring curiosity front and center in your own life.

As you will see, others challenged me to get out of my comfort zone. Trusted mentors—as well as untrustworthy people I definitely did *not* want to emulate—showed me the good, the bad, and the ugly.

My purpose is to share with you the most important insights I have garnered in a life full of adventure, new beginnings, painful endings, and the support of a circle of friends and family. This is your guidebook for staying ahead of change, for summoning up your curiosity in the face of agonizing decisions, and, above all, for living a full life causing change, surviving change, and thriving with change.

1

Change Is Not the Enemy

I REALIZED EARLY ON IN THE PROCESS OF GOING BLIND that I could not take myself too seriously.

I feel I am on top of the mountain, physically and metaphorically; I have a loving, harmonious family (OK, mostly harmonious); I've found the job of my dreams; I am in the best condition of my life and in great health; and after riding my bike to the top of one of Colorado's tall mountain passes, my riding buddies nickname me "van Hallinass."

If that were you, what would it take to shake your confidence and make you aware of your vulnerability? What would it take for your biking buddies never to use your clever new nickname again? What would it take to throw you off the mountaintop?

In my case, it took what happened the very next morning, after one of my steepest ascents ever.

It was a hot August morning. I woke up at 4:45 a.m., as I always did. I shuffled into the bathroom, looked into the mirror, and realized that I had lost my eyesight in the lower half of my right eye.

Imagine my terror. Two years earlier, I had awakened with the same symptom in my left eye. After several exhaustive tests, I was told I'd had a transient ischemic attack, or TIA, of my optic nerve—a mini stroke. I was assured that the damage was done and that I would never see from the lower half of my left eye again. I was urged to go on with my life, so I did. The next morning, I flew back to Argentina for a two-week family vacation. While there, I gradually lost the remaining eyesight in my left eye. Upon my return, after more exhaustive tests, I was once again told that the damage was done, but I was assured that the chances of my right eye being affected were ten billion to one.

I took the doctors at their word and went on with my life. Over the next two years, I proceeded to achieve new milestones as CEO of the large, historic Denver Athletic Club, watched with pride the growth and development of my children, improved my skiing skills, and racked up more than five-thousand miles annually on my bike.

Yes—the view from the top of the metaphorical and physical mountain was breathtaking. But on that fateful August 15, 2011, as I stood in front of the mirror, I realized with horror that it was all going to come crashing down to a whole new reality—I was going to be blind.

Hoping against hope, I drove to my optometrist, who, after several tests, referred me to another specialist, and so my day of reckoning began with the optometrist, an ophthalmologist, a retina doctor, and an optic nerve doctor. At 9:15 that night, I lay on a gurney in the emergency room at Littleton Adventist Hospital, with an intravenous drip pumping me full of steroids in a frenzied attempt to bring down the inflammation in my eye. I started the sudden descent into anger, self-pity, and despair. Would I be able to see the faces of my children and wife again? What about my job, cycling, and just basically getting along in life? With tears streaming from my eyes, I wanted to scream at the world: WHY ME? WHY THIS? I remember thinking that a diagnosis of cancer might have been more benevolent—anything but blindness.

I want to pause here to repeat: this book is not a competition for whose change is more profound or more difficult; it is an opportunity for you to reflect on what change is currently affecting your life. What is causing you to despair or lose sleep? Is it a missed promotion? A divorce? The birth of a child? Whatever the occasion, difficult or joyous, it is change. How are you facing it? Walk in my shoes for a moment and do some serious introspection on how you *choose* to handle the change. If you're like me, you might feel anger and despair; you may want to scream.

Yes, I felt those things, but suddenly, as I lay on the gurney, another thought invaded my mind. My eyes were so dilated from all of the tests during that long day, I wondered why they had brought me to the emergency room instead of to the baby delivery room.

Now, I know this was a strange thought, but it came unbidden into my mind, and it made me smile. Yes, I was worried about seeing my wife's and children's faces, my job, my cycling and so much more... but I *was* able to smile. My mind reminded me of a bad joke about dilating pupils. I laughed out loud.

The nurse wanted to know what was so funny, so I reluctantly shared the joke with her, and we laughed together. She called the other nurses over and I repeated the joke until the doctor came in wanting to know what the ruckus in her emergency room was all about. We started sharing other funny stories and began yukking it up, and I realized that my "darkness" was beginning to dissipate.

No, laughing had not cured me, but for a brief moment, my outlook had changed. Laughing had brought light to despair under the direst of circumstances.

Let's stop and think about it. Where would anger, despair, and wishing get you? Surely, it would fulfill the need to feel victimized—to wallow in self-pity. But in the end, all it does is leave you feeling angry, defeated, and depressed. Realize now that **change is not the enemy; the wrong attitude toward change certainly is**.

Here is where I wish to shine some light into your life. The change you are experiencing might be temporary or permanent, deep or shallow, easy or difficult, but the change itself is only the symptom; how it will affect your life is your choice. As a friend told me after one of my presentations: "Change is inevitable; personal growth is optional." Isn't that wonderful? You can run at the windmills all day long and get more and more frustrated, angrier, and consequently depressed, or you can choose to find the humor, to understand this change is not the universe aligning against you.

I get it. You want things to go back to the way they were. Well, so do I. But wishing will not make it happen. You need to evaluate whether returning to your old ways is realistic.

If you find yourself in the same situation I did, where the change cannot be reversed, then you have only two options:

You can channel all your energy into being a blocker, feeling sorry for yourself, moping, and basking in self-pity. Or you can roll up your sleeves and let curiosity help you put all your energy into becoming part of the change, into creating the world you envision and desire, not the one you were handed.

Yes, it is difficult—sometimes impossible—but you do have the choice. You can *judge* your situation by looking *backward*, using your prejudices and preconceived ideas to waste energy creating a toxic environment that sucks you in. Or you can *assess* the situation by looking *forward*, by discovering how you can learn, can change careers—can do whatever it takes not only to adapt but also to stay ahead of the change that is affecting you.

If You Always Do What You Always Did

You have probably heard this ancient Chinese saying, which perhaps is apocryphal: "May you live in interesting times."

Interesting times can be seen as a curse or a blessing. The monotony implied in an uninteresting time is certainly not something we should aspire to, but the chaos and confusion created by constant change may certainly make change feel like a curse, when everything around you seems to be in a constant state of flux and upheaval.

The old adage, "If you always do what you always did, you will always get what you always got," has worked for a very long time. For instance, a father might tell his son, "If you always plow our land the way I plowed it, you will always be able to provide for your family." And for centuries the only things that might have changed were the names of the horse and the son. However, in today's world where we replace our phones as frequently as every year, software no longer comes in boxes, and we summon a car with an app, we must constantly adapt to a new reality. If you always do what you always did, you are out of business.

For some of us, that new reality is truly exciting, but for others it is downright intimidating. We stick our heads in the sand and pretend we are living in uninteresting times. I remember that, as we started to transition from typewriters to desktop computers, many managers refused to learn to type. I watched the world leave them behind. The world will not wait for you to be ready for change.

CURIOSITY

Here is where curiosity is so important. You cannot move forward if you are stuck in an old frame of mind. I would really, really love to be sighted again, but reality tells me that—unless a new stem cell miracle cure comes out—I am out of luck. I was "fortunate" that my blindness was sudden and final. Why? By going blind within two weeks, I knew I was blind. Many blind people lose their eyesight very gradually, and it's difficult for them to determine when they've crossed the threshold from normal sight into true blindness. On which day will you decide, "OK, now I need a cane," or worse, "Today is the day I will stop driving forever"? For me, that day came six days after my diagnosis. It was one of the most difficult days of my transition. I knew when I went inside and told Nancy that I should not drive and turned in my keys, there would be no going back. Transitioning, however hard, was obvious to me in a way that isn't obvious for every person who gradually is going blind.

Perhaps the changes affecting you have come slowly, have taken many months or years, and you are now realizing that the situation has changed sufficiently to make it unbearable. Maybe yours is about a personal relationship, or a beloved software, or conditions in your neighborhood, or your health, and so on.

We all know the old fable about boiling a frog. It is no different for us. Gradual change lulls us into believing that our situation is not so bad, and we cope with it. That is why I believe sudden change is preferable: you know what you are faced with, you know the consequences, and you are forced to make a decision (or not). You know where you stand. Here is where curiosity will play a role in helping you understand that you do have choices. With gradual change, you have to be extra curious, and in some cases, you can only guess at the consequences you will face.

Take, for example, climate change. Just like the frog in increasingly hotter water, it is happening gradually, so we have skeptics who believe humans are not causing it and believe in waiting to see what will happen. However, the curious ones are projecting the *potential* of the danger and want to take action.

This is not about "taking sides." It's about letting the facts point you to a course of action and allowing your curiosity to let you revise your course based on new facts or data. By avoiding taking a strong position for or against a particular issue, but allowing the science and facts to reshape it, you remain open to change.

This is where the magic of curiosity comes in. Can you rescue the situation? How? Is it realistic? Or is it time to move on and be curious about alternatives? The purpose of this book is not to trivialize your situation, but to offer you the *choice* to grieve and feel sorry for yourself or open your eyes to alternatives.

When we lose a loved one, it is so easy to allow our sorrow to take us away, to hide from reality, to crawl under a rock. And yes, it feels good to feel bad. We may feel guilty, angry, and despondent and feel justified to withdraw into our darkness. And that, dear reader, is your choice. It may sound callous and cruel, but it is reality. Take that energy you are pouring into self-pity and do something constructive. As much as you wish it, the world will not be stopping for you.

When change happens as the result of a layoff or an accident, don't despair. Instead, be curious. The important thing to realize is that you have a choice. The sooner you make it, the better the chances of minimizing the effects on your happiness. You can choose to curse the darkness, or you can choose to light a candle.

Change is not the enemy.

2

The Pursuit of Happiness

WHEN OUR FOREFATHERS WROTE THE DECLARATION of Independence and penned the words that we "have the inalienable rights to Life, Liberty and the pursuit of Happiness," they unwittingly condemned us to the Pursuit of Happiness.

Think about it. When we pursue happiness, it becomes something we can never catch—it is always just out of reach.

How many times in our lives have we pursued happiness? When we were in middle school, we thought we would be truly happy and cool when we reached high school, or when we got a partner, or got a car, or got to college, or got the job … well, you get the drift.

So, why, you ask, do I talk about happiness in a book about Change and Curiosity?

Because too many times we allow, or expect, change to be the catalyst for happiness or unhappiness. Do you remember the time you bought that new car? How happy did it make you feel? Yes, you finally got the resources lined up, maybe after years of hard work, and it all paid off, and you drove off with the new car. You should feel *just as happy* every time you think of the new car you will be driving in the future, as you do every time you think of your new car in the present. It should be no different with your spouse—your wedding should not be the happiest day of your marriage. Every day leading to it, and every day after it, you have reasons to choose to be happy, or unhappy.

When I started my career in hospitality as a pot washer at the historic Hotel Vier Jahreszeiten in Hamburg, my roommate had just garnered a promotion to floor supervisor in room service, because he had put in the time and had received a diploma for his study of English. We went out to celebrate with his girlfriend and, during dinner, he asked her to marry him. I ordered a bottle of champagne (about a month's worth of my disposable income), toasted the couple, then proposed a toast "to French."

"Why French?" Richard asked.

"Well," I responded, "if English got you promoted to floor supervisor, French may get you promoted to manager."

"No!" Richard exclaimed. "I have the job I wanted, I got the girl I wanted ... I am happy! I am done."

It took me decades to understand how he could "settle" at such an early age. He had the whole world in front of him, but he was happy to accept what he had and not aspire for more. It was totally unfathomable to me. But now, as I look back, I realize how many sacrifices I have made to get where I am. The friends I left behind due to numerous job relocations, the long hours, the tough layoffs during downturns, the toll it has taken on my wife and children—could

I have been happy settling down at twenty-one?

The answer for me is a categorical NO! But who am I to judge Richard? He chose a path as different from mine as night is from day, but I am willing to bet that he has had every chance to be just as happy, if not happier, than I am.

Happiness is not dependent on change. Happiness is a state of mind that exists despite the changes, whether good or bad, that push your life forward.

We are the masters of our lives, and we can control how change affects us. Happiness should not be change-dependent. Happiness is something we are, or we are not. *We*—and not some purposeful, random, or disruptive event—are in charge.

Yes, granted, we get momentary satisfaction from achieving a goal, or we feel despair when something bad happens, but it is *our* responsibility to realize that the change that has brought this about should not dictate the long-term wellbeing and happiness of our lives.

HAPPINESS IS YOUR RESPONSIBILITY

In 1980, I graduated from hotel school and got my first job as director of quality at the Sheraton New York Hotel & Towers. ITT, the owner of Sheraton Hotels at the time, decided it was time to join the "quality movement," and I found myself implementing process improvements to every operation in this massive 1,800-room hotel. Change had come knocking, and I was supposed to be the catalyst.

One day, I found myself in front of the waitstaff of the hotel's coffee shop, explaining why we were introducing a new process of making sure that toast and muffins were served promptly after coming out of the toaster. Matty, a large African-American woman and feisty veteran of the trenches who had seen managers and processes come and go, stood up and argued, "Honey, I'm late with the rent, the landlord is looking to evict me, I'm raising my two grandchildren while my son sits in jail, my no-good bum of a husband gives me nothing but trouble, and you want me to worry about how crispy a $%^& muffin is?"

Stunned, it took me a moment to seize the opportunity, but I finally retorted that if she made every effort to make her customers happy, and even remarked to them, "Honey, I made sure your muffin is extra crispy," she would surely increase her tips. And that if we *all* did our best to ensure the total satisfaction of *every* guest, our hotel would always be busy, and we would not have to do seasonal layoffs. Matty was a hard woman, and life had made her bitter and angry, but she was smart and curious. She saw change coming and chose to grow from the experience. From that day on, she took me under her arm and helped me learn how to better address the team and how to truly "hear" them. And Matty always made sure I knew how crispy my muffin was.

Not everyone responds to change as Matty did. Take the movie, *A Dog's Purpose*, in which one of the main characters, Ethan, gets admitted to Michigan State on a full ride football scholarship but is seriously injured in a fire and loses the scholarship. He sees his dreams evaporate. He breaks up with his girlfriend. He leads an embittered life. Change came to him in the form of fire, injury, and the subsequent loss of his scholarship. His girlfriend was standing by him, but he wanted no comfort or handouts. He chose anger over happiness. His choice was *not* to grow from the experience but to find refuge in anger and self-pity. We *always* have a choice.

When I lost my eyesight, I certainly had all those feelings, and many more. Some of us can pull ourselves out of the dive quickly, others take a bit longer, but it is our job to pull ourselves out. Remember, you are the only one responsible for how the world perceives you. The ten most powerful two-letter words in the English language are: "If it is to be, it is up to me."

Happiness is your responsibility. If the change that disrupts your life is that you have been laid off, or served with divorce papers, or told you have but a year to live … does it mean that you must give up on happiness? Or that you must drown your despair in self-destructive practices? No! You have the power to become curious about how best to get beyond the situation, to learn to live with and adapt to your new reality, and to let the people around you see your strength and marvel at your happiness.

Would I love to see again? You bet! Would I love not to have cancer? Most certainly! I can beat cancer; I cannot recover my eyesight. While I am engaged in a battle against cancer, with side effects that are painful and disruptive, I am responsible for giving my life a purpose, a reason to get out of bed every morning. In spite of it all, I allow myself to be happy.

I am no different from you. Before losing my eyesight, I was so ignorant about blindness that I would have sworn I would despair if I ever became blind. But I learned to adapt, to persevere, and to thrive under the most trying of circumstances. And so can you—you have the strength inside you. You just have to be curious about how to bring it out.

Adapting is not about "attitude" or "aptitude"—it is about using your curiosity to choose to learn, to find the workaround, or to accept the situation and find a way to laugh, to grow, and yes, to help others go through what you have.

Wayne Gretzky is credited with having said, "You miss 100 percent of the shots you don't take." Get out there and take your shots. And know in your heart that every failure brings you one try closer to success.

Happiness is *not* goal oriented. Happiness is a state of mind. Change is omnipresent and therefore cannot be the catalyst for how you feel. *You* decide how you feel every day. Yes, goals are very important to get where you want to go in life, but you need to enjoy the process of achieving your goals as well as the fruits of the achievements, and (dare I say?) the failures, along the way.

Back to the Declaration of Independence. The next time you think about that famous phrase, be a bit dyslexic. Think of yourself as having "the inalienable right to Life, Liberty, and the Happiness of the Pursuit!"

3

Types of Change

NOW THAT WE HAVE EXPLORED HOW CURIOSITY HELPS impact change, let's get a little more familiar with change itself.

Change, in my view, comes in three variations, as I mentioned in the Introduction: Environmental, Purposeful, and Disruptive. Let's look at each of these more closely.

ENVIRONMENTAL CHANGE

Environmental change is the one that happens through natural causes and has been around since the beginning of time: we age, the weather destroys our crop, we get a nasty diagnosis. Science has both helped and hindered this type of change. We now live longer, age more gracefully, have remedies to illnesses that prevent their epidemic spread, and we benefit from cures that were unthinkable only a year ago. Conversely, our population is growing exponentially, the world's climate is rapidly changing, and we have invented weapon systems that can take out large populations at once.

How we respond to environmental change helps define us. Think about it: how many people do you know who have aged wonderfully and how many who are unwilling to change their way of life to help the aging process? Or people who react one way or another to a nasty diagnosis? I realize that this kind of change is many times very difficult to face. We cannot always see the bright side.

I believe that this is where curiosity plays a significant role. Are you curious about how to keep your body young? About how to deal with the health condition afflicting you? About how you could play a role in diminishing the impact of climate change? We *can* affect environmental change by focusing on the results we want to achieve. You don't have to accept the world the way it is. You can make it the way you visualize it. In the long run we will die, but how we get there is mostly up to us. And how we deal with change is how the world around us will perceive and remember us.

Environmental changes tend to be inexorable and resist outside influence. Because most of us do best when given a drastic hypothetical scenario, think of this one: you are given a year to live. Will you choose the road of darkness and despair for that year or the road of light? How you choose to deal with this scenario will determine how the world will deal with you. Be curious. Look for alternatives. Look at what positives there are, however hard they may be to find. Find the humor in your life.

Shortly after I was diagnosed with the same ailment in my right eye that would take my eyesight two weeks later, a mutual friend introduced me to Erik Weihenmayer. Erik is a climber who has summited the Seven Summits (the tallest mountains on each continent) and had just finished kayaking the Grand Canyon when I met him. He also happens to be blind. He invited me to go on a tandem bike ride with a couple of his friends as captains. When we stopped for lunch, he reminded me of something I will never forget: I am the very same person I had been a month earlier, only without one of my senses. That was such a wakeup call. I am who I am. I should not be defined by my lack of eyesight. Neither should you be defined by your age, by your health, or by your general wellbeing.

When I define environmental change as the type that "just happens," I know I run the risk of sounding fatalistic. My hope is to make sure you see that, with a curious attitude, you can combat the effects that environmental change could have on your life. That you do have the ability to choose either the path of darkness or the path of light. That we can slow down the progress of aging by exercising, eating the proper diet, and keeping our minds active. That we can choose how we will live our lives after a bad diagnosis. In short, happiness need not be hampered by environmental change.

PURPOSEFUL CHANGE

Purposeful change is the type of change that you—or someone else—intentionally sets out to make and that affects you. You work hard and get the promotion; you develop new software; a competitor puts you out of business. Although environmental change, as described above, certainly can have a purposeful component to it, with purposeful change, you have much more control in how you adapt. You are the one deciding where to take your life, how to shape your career, how fit you want to be, and so on. You are working hard toward earning a promotion when you suddenly get sick. Or your house is taken out by a tornado. These are environmental reasons to redouble your purposeful change efforts, rather than giving in to the fate of inevitability.

Purposeful change can be brought about by people who decide to improve on your invention, a spouse who decides to leave you, or a politician who changes the law that had previously allowed your business to exist.

All this means is that you need to redouble your efforts to be curious about how to overcome, adapt to, or vanquish the change. Be curious about why your spouse is ready to leave you, long before you reach that point. Be curious about how to build continuous improvement into your life and your business or job. Don't get stuck in the status quo. The old saying, "If it isn't broken, don't fix it," no longer holds true. If it isn't broken, then break it and put it together in a better way. Be a change agent, not a change victim.

When I worked at Hyatt Hotels & Resorts, we used to do Hyatt Talks, where Human Resources would invite ten random employees to have lunch (breakfast for the graveyard shift) with the general manager. Hyatt Talks had a dual purpose of having me get to know the line staff and having them get to know each other across departments that usually didn't interact. Most importantly, these talks gave me the opportunity to be curious about what was happening in their departments. We talked about what was not working. Were they missing supplies? We talked about our scheduling practices, pay issues, and so forth. We can all take steps like these within our organizations to gather the information that will allow us to make the right purposeful change.

Research and Development is all about purposeful change, right? R&D is the deliberate effort to explore the market for pricing, product placement, or training gaps, or for discovering a whole new product, just to name a few responsibilities. R&D is *all* about curiosity. Curiosity is elementary in getting a leg up on the competition. As you look into what is the best school for your child, the best car for your lifestyle and budget, the best treatment for your child's diagnosis, and even the best marriage counselor to salvage your relationship, you are exercising curiosity in the service of purposeful change.

That is, *you are being curious* about altering something in your life. The more you exercise your curiosity, the better chance you will have of preventing a disruptive change from turning your life upside down.

Create an environment where you and your team or your household are always open to change. You'll achieve that by being curious yourself, by listening, by reading, and by constantly challenging yourself to find a better way to do what you do. In my career, every evening when I took the trip home, I challenged myself to think of three ways I had made a difference that day. Could a similar approach help challenge you to be curious about new ways of thinking? Although monotony and predictability can give us a sense of security and continuity, guard against lulling yourself into believing that all is OK. Remember that your competitors are constantly striving to overtake you.

Understanding the power of purposeful change, whether done *by* you or *to* you, will help you realize how being curious, how opening your mind to wanting to understand what others are saying and doing and wanting to know how you can improve on the current way, should give you the tools to get ahead of change and be happy with the outcome. But now for the real benefit. Purposeful change will often be incremental. In today's world, incremental change is the price of entry. However, when you are open to adapting to and creating purposeful change, you are opening the windows and doors to disruptive change.

DISRUPTIVE CHANGE

Disruptive change can come from anywhere. An environmental change, such as a bad diagnosis, can certainly disrupt your life. A purposeful change from a subordinate who wants your job, a competitor who breaks into your market, or a spouse who decides to leave you, can and will be disruptors.

However, the goal of this book is to put you in the disruptor seat, and failing that, to help you see that when you are disrupted, it still is up to you to be curious about how you can pull it all together and decide what direction you need to go, so you can get back on top of your life. Disruption can ruin a plan or change your vision for your life, but disruption should not, by any means, derail your ability to be happy. Setbacks are a part of our lives. And *we* decide how they affect us emotionally, not the other way around.

The horseless carriage (the car) disrupted the horse industry, but that took several generations. The personal computer disrupted the typewriter industry, and that happened within one generation. Netflix disrupted Blockbuster, and that happened within a handful of years.

In 2007 when Steve Jobs announced the iPhone, the makers of BlackBerry, Research in Motion, were certainly curious. They acquired the new phone, took it apart, and carefully studied its components. They formed focus groups, gave them the phone to play with, and asked for their reactions. Their experts, along with most of us, came back with the conclusion that the keyboard was too hard to use. They (and we) loved the traditional physical keyboard and felt that the iPhone was not enterprise-friendly and was too fragile. Bloomberg commentator Matthew Lynn confidently predicted, "The iPhone is nothing more than a luxury bauble that will appeal to a few gadget freaks."

What went wrong?

Research in Motion was curious, right? They did take the phone apart, and they had focus groups. What else could they have done? I realize that I am a Monday morning quarterback, and that hindsight gives me the advantage. But, as an early adopter of the iPhone, I can say with confidence that they *judged* the iPhone, instead of *assessing* it (In Chapter 5 I'll share more about judging and assessing). They used their prejudice toward the physical keyboard and their preconceived ideas of how a phone should operate to reach the conclusion they did. Did they ask their tech department to visualize the future potential of the phone? Or what it might be like once it became more enterprise-friendly? Did they wonder what the second and third generations might look like?

Although the iPhone would probably have stolen significant market share from BlackBerry regardless, Research in Motion lost three crucial years in R&D that, in the end, cost them their perch at the top of the mountain.

Steve Jobs might not have been an easy man to be around, but he was one of the most brilliant disruptors of our era. He disrupted not only the telephone industry but also the movie industry, music industry, and book industry.

I do not think that we mere mortals can cause the kind of disruption that Steve Jobs did, but that should not stop us from striving to disrupt how things are currently done. You should be an avid consumer of information regarding your industry and the topics that affect your life. Attend seminars and industry events and watch your competition closely. Be curious about what your team is thinking, particularly that new employee—or your spouse. Create an environment where people are rewarded for bringing forward new ideas and assess the potential game changers in your life.

Environmental, Purposeful, and Disruptive changes are just names to help classify stages of change, but as we have seen, they have significant overlap. Although there is a certain inevitability to change, it need not be a crusher of our goals and ambitions. With curiosity, we can and should be able to discover an alternative to whatever change comes at us. Above all, stay a step ahead of change. Instead of being disrupted, become a disruptor!

4

Are You Asking Questions?

THE HEART OF CURIOSITY IS ASKING QUESTIONS—NOT only of your spouse, children, or team members but also of yourself. Too many times, we allow the automatic response to previous similar situations to stop us from fully evaluating the present one.

Are you curious about where your children want to go on vacation? Most times, we plan the trip then announce it to our children. But what if we asked them? Yes, they might say "Disney World!" and, when the reality of your bank account sinks in, all you can do is a "staycation." You owe them an explanation, and if it is not to be, then it is up to you and your spouse to explain the reality of the family finances. But the change of plans does not mean that you have not *heard* them. Maybe you decide to save a little every year, and in five years you finally take the family to Disney World (provided that their wishes have not changed).

Curiosity will help you keep a clear channel of communication between family members, subordinates, associates, and clients.

One of the key ways to demonstrate your curiosity in the workplace is to practice "management by wandering around." Stop and have a frank conversation with line staff and middle management. Find out about each of them as a person, rather than just getting a recap of yesterday's game. Then ask them pointed questions about the inner workings of their department: What is working what could use some tweaking or improvement, and above all, how do they feel about their job? Would they recommend their job to their best friend? Are they planning to stay? What is their vision for the future?

When I was the rooms executive at the Radisson Hotel in Alexandria, Virginia, my general manager came to tell me that the brakes on van no. 3 were squealing. I asked him how he had found out, and he told me that Tommy the bellman (and driver) had told him. I thanked the GM and wrote the work order to have the brakes checked. I then went looking for Tommy and, after thanking him for making us aware of the issue, asked him why he had told the general manager and not me about the brakes. (My question was potentially damaging because I put Tommy on the defensive.) His response? "HE ASKED."

What a revelation. I assured Tommy that he had done the right thing. I promised him that, in the future, I would make sure to ask. I also encouraged him to make sure that he reported issues on his own without being asked.

Earlier, I mentioned Hyatt Talks, a practice of me, as general manager, meeting with ten random employees for breakfast or lunch in one of the hotel's restaurants. We would go around the table and tell a little bit about ourselves, our background, where we were from, education, hobbies, family, and so on. This enabled us to find out more about each other. When you go into the cafeteria of any organization, you typically see people sitting down with coworkers from within the same department. By allowing a housekeeper to find out a little bit about the personal life of a cook, we may create an environment where in the future they will choose to sit together in the cafeteria but, more importantly, they may be more motivated to cooperate and work together should the need arise.

At these gatherings, I would then ask each person about his or her workplace, practices, supplies, tools, training, and boss. I would take careful notes and promise to get back to them with resolutions. I would then share the feedback with my executive team. This is a very delicate step. You have to assure your team that when you are sharing this feedback with them, you are on *their* team, that this is not a "gotcha." The employee then has to hear how we are going to proceed. It is critical that, as the information moves down the organization chart, every level of management feels that we are helping them, rather than meddling with their department. We insisted that every manager thank the employee in question and involve him or her in creating the solution.

One time, many years after I had left Hyatt, I was describing to a fellow general manager how I had continued to use this practice throughout my career. He was shocked and dismayed that I would do so. His concern was, for example, if a housekeeper told me that we were short on sheets, and we did not have the money in the budget to buy sheets that month, how would we handle that?

It is funny how sometimes we can be so shortsighted on such

a simple issue. Don't the hidden costs of not having enough sheets far surpass the cost of buying new sheets? If the housekeepers leave housekeeping with empty carts, we now have to divert the housemen from their regular duties and convert them to linen runners, so they can bring linen up to the housekeepers. The laundry must work overtime to turn the sheets over, and housekeepers are unhappy because they cannot complete their tasks on time and might be late picking up the kids from school. Arriving guests are disappointed that rooms are not ready for early arrivals, and overall morale suffers.

What hidden costs are you ignoring? How are you being short-sighted by lacking the curiosity to go out and seek the information that will streamline your operation? What blind spots are you ignoring?

There are many management tools to help us with measuring the level of engagement and commitment to the job, such as associate surveys, informal chats with staff, anonymous notes, and so on. They cannot replace your personal curiosity for each employee you encounter. Although associate surveys have a terrific purpose, they are spaced apart and lack the personal touch of the boss showing that she cares about them as a person as well as a contributor to the bottom line. This is not something that will happen overnight, but your wandering around asking questions will create an atmosphere of sharing and participating. When employees tell you about a deficiency or issue, it is important that their immediate supervisor does not inadvertently or deliberately make them feel guilty, because they will never speak up again.

Get out there! Talk to your employees, spend a couple of hours every day wandering around so employees and the management team get used to seeing you. You will begin to notice that they will start emulating you. Slowly but surely, you will have created an environment where people feel safe and comfortable sharing ideas and being curious about better outcomes.

LISTEN

The other side of asking questions, of course, is to listen to the answers we get.

The old adage, "God gave us two ears and one mouth, so listen twice and speak once," is crucial in stoking your curiosity. Most times, when we think we are listening, in reality we are postulating our response to the other person's point of view, idea, or concern. Rather than hearing what they are saying, we are busy throwing up barriers to their ideas. There is no faster way to kill ideas than by not really listening.

In my job as CEO of the Denver Athletic Club, one of the departments was a fully licensed childcare center. We were licensed for 120 children from infant through preschool, and the DAC was at full capacity due to a critical scarcity of downtown childcare centers. Our waiting list exceeded a gestation period!

Shortly after I started my job, Maria, one of the instructors, came to see me and told me how excited she was that we "finally have one of us [an Hispanic] for a boss." She then proceeded to tell me that in her room we were "over capacity and under ratio." I had no idea what she meant, so I asked her to please explain it to me. Essentially, we had too many babies for the capacity of the room and not enough caregivers to comply with the rules on the ratio of babies to caregivers.

I clearly heard her, apologized, and thanked her profusely. I then called Maria's direct supervisor and shared Maria's concern. The immediate response was that Maria was a "problem employee" who had an issue with everything they tried. She promised to speak with Maria and get back to me. I then called the division head and told her how I had talked with Maria and with her department head. The division head's response was similar: Maria was a problem employee, and they would handle the situation.

Two weeks later, an inspector from the Department of Health and Human Services showed up in my office, claiming she had received a complaint regarding the ratio and capacity of our infant room. We were indeed in violation and would have to reduce the number of babies by Friday of that week.

What went wrong here? I had listened to and heard Maria, yet I had failed to bring about the necessary change. From Maria's perspective, we had not only ignored her, but we had also made her the source of the problem.

If I had truly been interested in her concern, I could have asked her to bring me the roster of how many babies we had in her classroom; the schedule, so I could determine how many staff members were scheduled; the room capacity; and the rules. With those readily available documents, in five minutes Maria could have set me straight. Instead, I chose to call her bosses, relay her concerns, and accept their judgment of the situation.

Although we indeed had many babies registered, many were registered for part-time childcare. We did not expect all parents of part-time babies to show up on the same days. But the reality proved Maria right; we simply had too many babies registered. The intention was to help desperate parents, but the practice was unfair to the caregivers and violated the law.

Maria had to work up her courage to go two levels above her position before she came to see me. That should have been enough to trigger my curiosity to investigate further. Instead, I allowed the judgment of Maria's supervisors to satisfy my curiosity and failed to assess the situation. I trusted the center director and her division director implicitly, and that is the way it should be. But trusting does not mean that, under the right circumstances, I should not double-check something.

This is the heart of a curious mind. Don't settle for the way you always did it. Ask yourself if there is a better way. Encourage your team members to challenge the status quo and encourage everybody around you to adopt a curious mentality. You will be surprised at how "new thinking" will start to take form all around you, and above all, in your own mind.

5

Assessing Versus Judging

YOU ARE PROBABLY THINKING YOU CANNOT POSSIBLY double-check everything that happens in your department, organization, or family. That is true. But the adage that "you get what you inspect, not what you expect" holds true. The lesson I learned from the events around our childcare center at the Denver Athletic Club was that when I allow my (or someone else's) prejudices and preconceived ideas to cloud my judgment, I fail to fully assess the situation. I allowed the judgment of the supervisor and director of one of the employees to influence me, and therefore I *judged* the situation (used prejudices and preconceived ideas; e.g., "Maria is a problem employee") instead of *assessing* the situation (asking Maria to provide the relevant documentation).

In the October 2017 issue of *Forbes* magazine, the article "How to Apply the Pope Francis' Leadership Principles to the Boardroom" had many valuable ideas. My favorite concept was where the Pope extolled us to "Don't judge; assess."

It is innate for us to judge a situation based on our past experiences, preconceived ideas, and prejudices. That is what judging means. You are looking backward to your past experience and acquired filters to formulate decisions about a person or situation. Because I had known no blind people when I lost my eyesight, my judgment about blindness was framed in ignorance. My initial terror at existing in a world of darkness was not grounded in fact but on assumptions. In the words of Pope Francis, "Who am I to judge?" By that, I believe he meant that we should not judge people, situations—or ourselves.

When I received my initial diagnosis of NAION (non-arteritic anterior optic neuropathy), my first reaction was one of panic, anger, denial, and yes, self-pity. In retrospect, those emotions are all natural, and it is important to go through the grieving process, but I could have come out of it a lot sooner had I taken the time to be curious about what blindness is. I had met only one other blind person in my fifty-seven years, and he was such an overachiever that he had climbed the Seven Summits while being totally blind. Erik Weihenmayer did not fit my image of blindness, and I totally discounted my chances of being like him, a man recognized as a climber who happens to be blind, not the other way around. Too many times we identify ourselves with our weaknesses, rather than our strengths.

It is sad how ignorance about something will make us jump to conclusions that come from judging the situation, rather than assessing it. My ignorance of blindness "made" me feel a lot worse about my future than I needed to be. What are you ignorant about? What is it you are judging? Is it your child, an employee, a new law?

Invest the time to satisfy a curious mind, then you will have the ability to assess the situation accurately, but only if you also have an open mind.

It was my friend Jack Barker who began to wake up my curiosity by telling me about the Colorado Center for the Blind, where they teach the visually impaired how to carry on a normal existence in spite of their blindness. Although I would have had to give up my job to be able to attend the school, as they operate during the day (eight hours a day for six months), that intense schedule clearly showcased the tremendous learning curve I would have to overcome. Jack also told me about a store that sold all the tools for helping the blind function efficiently.

When we went to the store and I saw all the video magnifiers, document readers, and talking watches and phones, and the plethora of canes, I began to comprehend the enormity of the transformation I would have to undertake to begin to adapt to my new reality.

I grabbed one of the canes and started walking around the store, swinging it in front of me as I had seen so many blind people do. The clerk came over and said, "You must be new at this," to which I responded, "Well, yes ... what gave me away?" He replied that canes are used to find obstacles. The way I was walking and swinging the cane right in front of me, if it found an obstacle, it would change the pitch of my voice as the cane collided with my body.

That experience is, in fact, what woke up my curiosity about how to transition into blindness. Instead of concentrating on what I would *not* be able to do, I concentrated on how to overcome blindness. Remember that, at this point, I was still sighted, albeit from one eye only, with diminished and weakening acuity. By having something to pour my energy into, by wanting to understand how to do things so I could move around the house, get to work, and keep my job, I was able to bring about the most significant change in my life.

I am not saying that I did not have moments of despair, self-doubt, anger, and frustration. They were plentiful and made the transition that much more difficult. But I was able to focus on what I needed to change to adapt, slowly but surely becoming more and more curious about overcoming the obstacle, rather than dwelling on what I could not do. In other words, I began the process of assessing my potential, rather than judging my shortcomings.

Imagine waking up every morning, and "forgetting" that you are blind. You open your eyes to turn off the alarm clock, only to realize that you can't see it. For a moment you hope it is all a bad dream. Then reality sinks in. You remember the last few days, the doctors, the injections in the eyeballs, the dilations, the tests, the diagnosis. You remember giving up the keys to your car, the realization that you no longer can read a profit and loss statement, that you can't see your children or wife. The darkness comes down with such force that it crushes your will to get out of bed.

The reality of my situation was aggravated by my judgment about my potential. However, when I assessed the situation, based on firsthand knowledge from contact with blind people, becoming educated on the subject and understanding the limitations of my loss of eyesight, I concluded that there was a lot I could do—as a matter of fact, nearly everything.

Through Eyecycle Colorado and Guide Dogs for the Blind, I met people who worked for large corporations or for the IRS, who owned their businesses, and so much more. And yes, I met people living off disability checks under the cloud of defeat. But mostly, I was exposed to people who led "normal" lives and who saw blindness only as something to overcome, not as an insurmountable barrier.

One such inspiration is Trevor Thomas, a man who is blind and who walked the Colorado Trail, among several other trails, with his guide dog, Tenielle. Others included a blind judge, a blind mobility trainer, and even a blind Ms. Colorado Senior America. Nothing stood in their way. For Erik Weihenmayer, not even Mount Everest.

OK, so if I rafted the Grand Canyon today, as I did seven years ago, I would not see the unbelievable vistas that magical place has to offer. But does that mean that I can't ever raft the Grand Canyon again? No, it just means that I will experience its majesty in a different way. Invariably, I have people describing what is around me. Granted, it is not the same as seeing it firsthand, but it certainly leaves a lot to my imagination—the picture that I think in my mind just might be superior to the one that nature offers.

Do You Judge?

Are you judging your child, spouse, boss, or subordinates? We tend to judge people based on past experience, other people's judgments, and even our past experiences with people "like" them. In our gut, we tend to judge people from the North or the South differently, women from men, immigrants from U.S. citizens, etc. Although some generalities might apply to each one of these groups, leading us to falsely judge them as individuals, it is in their individuality that they stand so differently from our preconceived ideas.

You might see your child as "stuck in her ways" and so not realize that she is changing every single day. When you judge her based on her past performance, you're being judgmental. However, if you assess her full potential and start treating her according to what she can be as opposed to what she is, you might be surprised at the change you will see in her.

It is no different if that relationship is with your boss, a difficult subordinate, or even your spouse. When you are judgmental, you are nothing more than the sum of your past experiences. As you find the fault and disappointment in people, places, situations, and so on, you start to form ideas about all of them and tend to call that "wisdom." And when you use that "wisdom" as opposed to your curiosity about their point of view, reasoning, and thinking, you are being judgmental. Open your mind to being curious about the other person's point of view. Explore their thoughts. Challenge their thinking with an open mind, wanting to understand their point of view as opposed to being intent on proving them wrong. It is only through that curiosity that you can truly expand your mind and be open to new ideas.

What is the change you are facing now? The one that keeps you up at night, the one that is having you ignore all the signs, and that is happening all around you? When you bury your head in the sand, you are typically being judgmental, only seeing the past and your preconceived ideas of outcomes.

Do you have the curiosity to explore alternative outcomes? For that, you will need to *assess* the situation. Explore what caused it (or what will cause it) and the points of pain, then imagine other possible outcomes.

When I judged my blindness, I was paralyzed by self-pity and therefore could not see the endless possibilities of existing as a blind man. By assessing, I was able to understand that, yes, it would be different; yes, it would be difficult; and yes, I would hate not seeing. But now I had given myself the opportunity to go beyond all the negative results. I was able to understand—if not for me then for my family—that I needed to summon the strength to overcome the difficulties. To understand that if I wanted to continue to be respected, I had to respect myself. That blindness is nothing to be ashamed of. But above all, that to make a successful transition, I would have to learn all new skills.

I am sure you would prefer to not have lost that account, or lost a spouse to divorce, or realized too late that your competitor beat you by being more innovative. In some cases, you are left with nothing to do but pick up the pieces. That is the very moment in which you need to assess whether you want to fight to try to salvage the relationship or the account or if you need to move on. Either way, you have to take action. And that action comes from being curious about outcomes. Some are very painful (how would you like to be a taxi driver in the face of Uber competition?), but taking no action—not being curious—will only take you deeper and deeper down the drain.

JUDGING KEEPS YOU ON THE COUCH

After I lost my eyesight, my friend Tim, a twenty-three-time Boston marathon runner, called to challenge me to ride the Elephant Rock bike ride. This is a "century ride," a 100-mile ride through beautiful Castle Rock, Colorado. In my mind, there was no way I was giving up control and relegating myself to the "stoker" (back seat) position on a tandem bike. After all, I was the CEO, and I was used to being in charge. It was not just the concern about putting my trust in someone else; deep down it was also my *need* to be in control, to be in charge. I turned Tim down.

As I sat on the couch at home, I quickly realized that my need to be in charge was clouding my decision—I could sit on the couch all day long or, if I released that need, I could once again be feeling the burn in my legs, the sweat running down my back, and the exhilaration of the wind in my face. My judgment that I *had* to be in charge was depriving me of the opportunity to remain active, enjoy Colorado's great outdoors, and deepen my friendship with Tim. When I put my prejudices and preconceived ideas aside, I was able to clearly see that the alternative, although not ideal, was truly my only option to continue to enjoy bike riding. Yes, being a stoker is certainly not the same as riding your own bike, but the reality is that I was no longer able to ride my bike. So why was I being so obstinate?

What are you being obstinate about? Are you willing to see that reality might have changed, and that if you don't compromise, you are going to be left behind? How about my friend Tim? He was willing to up the freedom of riding his bike, at his pace, whenever he wanted, wherever he wanted, to give me the opportunity to get off the couch and get outside. But, blinded by my petty, preconceived ideas, I refused to see that Tim was sacrificing a lot more than I was to give me this opportunity. How many times do we fail to see that the people around us are reaching out to help, because we are too proud, too stuck in our ways to understand that we need to open our minds and assess the situation?

By opening your eyes to alternative outcomes, you will be moving from judging to assessing. Have fun imagining how you will reinvent yourself, your organization, and your life to meet or beat impending changes. Stay ahead of the curve. Stop having an open-door policy with a closed mind!

6

Pride, the Need for Control, and Communication

ONE OF THE OBSTACLES WE HAVE WHEN FACED WITH change, and which curiosity can help us overcome, is our own pride.

The day I was diagnosed with the disorder that would take my eyesight within two weeks, I found out that if I wanted to learn to use the white cane, I would have to go to the Division of Vocational Rehabilitation. There, they would assign me a caseworker who in turn would assign me to a trainer. Wow, me? A caseworker? NO WAY! I am a *giver*, not a *taker*! I rejected the idea—until I realized that the only way I could get trained on how to use a white cane was to follow those steps.

In the meeting with my caseworker, she marveled that even though I was still sighted, I was there seeking instruction. She told me she has clients who have been blind for more than five years and are still in denial. My "advantage" was that I became blind suddenly. Losing your eyesight gradually makes it truly difficult to decide on what day you pronounce yourself blind. In my Bible study group, we had been discussing what it means to be humble. One of the definitions we settled on was "having the ability to accept help." Reflecting on that discussion helped me. I had to go through a process of first accepting that I now lived in an altered reality, then accepting there was no going back to the way things were.

PRIDE

Are you going through a gradual change right now and, like those clients at the Division of Vocational Rehabilitation, simply accepting those small changes as part of your life but ignoring the big picture? At what point will you act? Incremental changes around you are lulling you into a false sense of security you should not be feeling. You need to be the change agent. Seize the initiative and assess, as best you can, what the full impact of the incremental changes will be. Like the person who is slowly going blind, one day you might wake up and realize that your marriage is over, or your health is beyond help, or your job is beyond salvaging.

Erik Weihenmayer told me clearly that I needed to realize I was the same man I was before losing my eyesight and never to "lose sight" of that fact. I had only lost one of my senses.

My insight was that I could use help, not only from my wife and my white cane trainer but from others as well. I was floored when my executive team took it upon themselves to write a letter to my employer's board of directors to let them know that each member of the team was standing behind me and would help pick up the slack in areas where my eyesight would prevent me from doing my usual work.

I was surrounded by people eager, even desperate, to help me, and yet at first I obstinately thought I could do it alone. It took many mornings of waking up to the reality of my blindness to realize that my life had indeed changed, and that if I was to take action, the time was now. I was living through the difficulty of environmental change and falling into the role of victim. It felt *good* to feel sorry for myself—to bask in the misery of my perceived future prospects without having to marshal the strength to make purposeful changes in my life that would allow me to move forward.

Don't make the same mistake. Allow your friends, colleagues, and family to give a helping hand. Become curious about alternative outcomes. Explore how much *you* need to change to adapt to the new reality.

When I entered third grade, I was a year ahead of others my age, but then I missed an entire year of school because of poor health and was required to repeat the year. My parents transferred me to a private British, all-boys school, where I was a full head shorter than the next boy. Our sports were rugby and soccer. I was terrible at both. I wore laced-up shoes while the other boys wore loafers. I wore my hair as mandated by the rulebook while the others pushed the limits. I raised my hand (a lot), and so much more. So yes, I was different, and the boys hazed me brutally to get me to bend to their ways.

I steadfastly refused, standing rigidly in the middle of the proverbial raging river, unbending, being battered by the current, the cold, and everything else the river had to throw at me. At one point, with tears in my eyes, I begged my father to let me go to another school. I will never forget his response. He pointed out that this was the first major problem I'd had in my life, and there I was, asking my father to resolve it for me. He challenged me to resolve the issue myself.

In retrospect I am proud that I stayed true to myself, but I have to acknowledge that the years that could have been some of the best of my life were marred by a miserable situation. Because I lacked curiosity, I allowed this to be one of the most difficult times of my life. I was not willing to consider confronting the bullies or changing some of the behaviors that set me apart.

I am not saying that I should have started to smoke to fit in or pick on another unfortunate boy to get the bullies off my back. I realize now that standing rigidly as I did took a serious toll on my happiness. I allowed a situation to decide for me how I would feel. Could I have confronted the nastiest of the bullies to get the others to back off? Could I have sat in the middle of the class instead of the front? Could I have compromised even a little bit?

So, blinded by my fierce determination to not give in, I missed out on the opportunity to find common ground, or at least to contemplate alternatives other than fleeing the school.

My father told me that if I changed schools, I would not change. I would be the same me wherever I was. I could not outrun me. If I wanted the hazing to stop, I would have to change!

Louis Zamperini, made famous by the book and movie *Unbroken*, had a clear purpose for his resistance to the Japanese in World War II. He was an example of resilience that inspired not only his fellow prisoners but also many of the guards in the POW camps—not to mention the millions of us who now know his story.

In his case, resistance and stubbornness, however painful and dangerous, had a purpose. In our own personal and professional lives, being willing to contemplate compromise sometimes is not only an advantage, but in many cases is necessary to achieve a common goal. Stop thinking that you are being a role model by not compromising and begin to explore, with an open mind, what the alternatives could be.

COMPROMISE AND COMMUNICATION

After I reconsidered my position about riding as stoker with Tim in the Elephant Rock century ride, I bought a tandem bike. I called Tim and we set the date for our first training ride. I was so excited to get riding that when Tim arrived, all I wanted to do was get on the road. Tim, however, wanted to know all about the gears (the bike has twenty-seven), the disc brakes, how we would communicate, and so on. I grew impatient but realized quickly that Tim and I had different management styles. Tim was more deliberate; I was more intuitive. If I wanted Tim to come back for a second ride, and if I ultimately wanted to do the century ride, I would have to learn to become curious about his style and be willing to compromise.

When you are involved in a merger, an acquisition, or with a new boss or a new life partner or spouse, do you find yourself needing to be in control? Do you find it difficult to compromise? You see, I had no choice: I could either compromise and learn to work with Tim, or I could go back to sitting on the couch. If you are not curious about the other person's point of view, you will destroy the ability to work harmoniously together. However, as I will depict below, compromising should not be a one-way street.

Soon after we got on the bike path and had the basics settled, I could not keep up with the pace Tim was setting, so I told him that he was "in the wrong gear." Tim's response was, "What do you mean, the wrong gear?" Tim preferred faster pedaling in lower gears with their low resistance and higher revolutions; I was used to the opposite: higher gears that require slower pedaling while applying more strength. We were riding in Tim's ideal cadence, but I was struggling to keep up. So now, if Tim wanted me to contribute to the pedaling on the long ride, it was *his* turn to listen and compromise. We learned that even though Tim was in charge, he needed to be curious and communicate with me to make sure that the pace he set was one that would challenge me, but not one that would wring me out in the first few miles.

Whether you are the supervisor or the subordinate, having a clear line of communication is vital to achieve forward motion and an ongoing, productive relationship. I have seen so many cases where a supervisor sets such a brutal pace for the team that it creates dissatisfaction, burnout, and, as a result, high turnover. Yes, it is satisfying to know that you have the knowledge and capability to push your team, but you also need to realize what their capabilities are. With training and a little bit of time—and a healthy dose of curiosity—you will be able to increase the pace, as Tim and I did on the tandem, but you have to work together to get to that point. Communication and compromise need to go both ways.

Close your eyes for a moment and picture a tandem bike where both riders are sitting back-to-back, facing in opposite directions, and pedaling as hard as they can. So many times I have seen teams working this way. The battle for forward momentum is hard, as each member of the team fully believes that he or she is working as hard as possible to contribute to the endeavor, but because they lack curiosity about each other's direction and are working against each other, they aren't getting anywhere.

Think about where you are "sitting on the couch" about a specific position you are stubbornly sticking to. This can happen with a couple, with a team, or in a supervisor-subordinate relationship. I do not want to be on a tandem; I would most certainly prefer to ride a bike on my own. But riding alone is no longer a possibility. So I have to compromise. And in many cases, so do you. Stop clinging to the way it was, wishing for things to go your way. Give up your pride and give up your need for control.

Tim and I rode the Elephant Rock successfully. During the final fifteen miles, riding north into the wind, Tim announced that we were "pulling a train" of more than thirty riders all the way to the finish line. We were proud of our accomplishment but, above all, we were proud of our teamwork.

Now imagine the captain and stoker on the tandem are the Republicans and Democrats in Congress, respectively. Both Republicans and Democrats are patriots. Each side fervently believes they are doing what is best for our country, for their party, and for their constituents. However, the bike hardly moves forward. It is good to know what you believe in and to fight for it, but are you curious about the other's point of view? Are you willing to give up some of your beliefs to achieve a compromise?

How can we expect Congress to compromise if we are unwilling to compromise in our own homes and at work? Our elected officials are "stuck" working with the group we elected to represent us. But we court and propose to our spouses, looking for a perfect match. True, we mature at different paces, our interests may begin to diverge, our jobs could place undue strain on our marriage, as could money, children, and so on. But these are all changes—and how should we deal with change effectively? By now, you know the answer: wake up your curiosity, find out your partner's point of view, and, just as Tim and I had to compromise, be prepared to give in. It is OK to push each other but not to the point where one is left behind. Forward motion will come to a gear-grinding halt.

Riding a tandem bike is certainly a huge compromise from riding my own bike. But it is a huge leap forward from sitting on the couch.

WHAT MOUNTAIN ARE YOU CLIMBING?

On that initial ride, after Tim and I finally figured out what a good cadence was for both of us, we faced the short but steep climb of Chatfield Dam near Denver. We argued all the way to the top, because we both needed to figure out what our best climbing gear was. Thank goodness this climb was short! It is no different in your life. As you embark on that new relationship, things seem to be going great, but then "life happens," and you face a climb that could be as short as Chatfield Dam, as tall as one of the Colorado fourteeners (mountains that are 14,000 feet tall), or as formidable a mountain as K2 on the China-Pakistan border.

Not quite a year after losing my eyesight, I lost my CEO job. A year later, I was diagnosed with a nasty melanoma that later metastasized. I guess these would *each* qualify as a K2! I was faced with significant disruptive changes that would require enormous introspection and assessment.

I most certainly did not wish to lose my job, and most definitely did not expect to get cancer. But the reality is that I did lose my job and I did get cancer. What K2, fourteener, or dam are you facing now? Each can seem insurmountable, but they are only as scary as you choose to make them. Yes, you might be scared, concerned, or even excited, as the change in your life might come in the form of a promotion for which you fear you may not be quite ready or in the form of a trip to a destination that has held a certain mystique for you. Whatever the change, you can adjust how it affects you by allowing your curiosity to take over.

7

Humility Goes a Long Way

DO YOU SOMETIMES GET THE FEELING THAT YOU, AND only you, know how to solve an issue? That everybody around you is being obtuse? If only they had listened to you. Isn't it great to know that you have a curious mind that helps you see things others don't? When I was diagnosed with my blindness, I *knew* how bad my life would be. I knew that I would no longer be able to function in society—and, above all, I knew that it was *my* battle. No one else could help me. In the process, I pushed my loved ones and the people who most cared about me far away. Is that "knowledge" healthy? How about exhibiting some humility and allowing the world to extend a helping hand?

Once I became adept in the use of the cane, I felt competent enough to go to work and perform my (albeit diminished) daily routines. One of the major changes we had to make was selling our beloved home of fifteen years in a neighborhood full of friends, so we could move closer to town and public transportation. That was a major sacrifice and a difficult change for both my wife and me. As we settled in and began to adapt to our new life, I started to become active within the blind community by attending a couple of meetings of the National Federation of the Blind (NFB) chapter in Colorado. Then I joined Eyecycle, a group that owns fourteen tandem bikes and gets blind people active in the great Colorado outdoors. Friends of friends would insist that I meet their visually impaired friends. All of these activities, plus my involvement with the Division of Vocational Rehabilitation, exposed me to guide dog users.

Another Way

How many blind friends do you have? When I was diagnosed with NAION and was told I would be blind in two weeks, I panicked. Part of my angst came from my total ignorance about blindness.

Nancy and my lovely daughter Anneke encouraged me to explore the possibilities of getting a guide dog, and I later found out that a group of my friends considered acquiring a guide dog for me, under the belief these dogs had to be purchased.

My pride kept me stubbornly opposed to getting a dog, rather than being curious about what having one could do for me. I saw the choice as either forcing me to be dependent on a guide dog or being able to fend for myself and maintain my independence using my cane. My cane was accomplishing everything I needed, and I did not have to take it outside to walk it, feed it, or relieve itself—so I pushed all my friends' encouragements aside. Full of pride, I stubbornly refused to see another way.

Then one day at an NFB meeting for guide dog users, I heard someone explain that we use our canes to *find* obstacles, but guide dogs help us *avoid* obstacles. What a revelation that was!

My new friends with guide dogs were able to navigate streets much faster than I did using my cane. Plus they had the benefit of wonderful companions. My stubbornness had prevented me from understanding that there were alternatives. Just because I had found one solution did not mean it was the *best* solution.

There is a powerful metaphor here. Do you go through life as though you have a cane, probing in front of you trying to find obstacles, or do you use a metaphorical guide dog that helps you anticipate and avoid obstacles? Granted, there are many blind people who can outpace me with their canes, but they have years and years of experience I lack. The point is that just because you found one solution, you should never stop being curious and never stop exploring alternatives. Try to "see" that sometimes a better alternative may be staring you in the face—if you only could be humble enough to recognize it.

IT'S EASY TO GET STUCK

I remember when I was working at a hotel in the early 1980s in New York City, and computers had begun to displace typewriters. I had bosses who stubbornly refused to learn to use computers, insisting that they were perfectly happy with the status quo. I was lucky that early in life I had taken typing lessons—on an old Underwood manual typewriter—and later became the telex operator at the famed Ritz Hotel in Paris. Knowing how to type, combined with my curiosity about new technologies, made my transition to the personal computer much smoother. But those executives who insisted the status quo was fine were rapidly marginalized or had to face a much steeper learning curve as their secretaries were replaced by PCs on their desks. The future was staring them in the face, yet their pride caused them to look the other way, stubbornly clinging to the past.

It was with that very same resistance that I had rejected the thought of a guide dog. Although I am not saying that dogs are the answer for every blind person (most blind people do incredibly well with their canes), I now understand that the dogs offer an alternative that makes life a lot easier for many people.

When I began my research on how to buy a guide dog, I looked online for suppliers in Denver, then in Colorado. I quickly discovered there are only nine guide dog schools in the United States—and you don't "buy" a guide dog. You're "matched" with a dog, and you must participate in the conclusion of its training.

Many of my new guide dog user friends had dogs from Guide Dogs for the Blind in San Rafael, California, so I went online and filled out the application, a very lengthy process. I had to wait for my application to be reviewed and accepted. After that, I had to send letters from my eye doctors explaining my condition and justifying my need for a dog. I also needed a note from my doctor stating that I was healthy enough to walk with a dog.

Next, we scheduled a phone interview that lasted more than an hour, in which they explored everything about me, from where I live to what I do, my health, my aspirations, and why I wanted a dog. After that, they scheduled a personal visit from one of their evaluators. She went over much of the previous information then asked me to take a walk with my cane that would take me a mile away from my home, crossing at least one major intersection.

The goal with this vetting process was to make sure I had the cane skills to navigate streets and crossings. Many people assume that the dog will take over those responsibilities, but (as you will find out) that is not so. Then the evaluator produced a harness and proceeded to explain the basic commands, such as stop (slow down to a stop), halt (stop immediately), left, right, and forward. She then grabbed the harness by the collar and told me I had to pretend she was a dog named Juno (this imaginary dog name is used by all the guide dog schools). She gave me the handle of the harness and told me to have her guide me home.

"Go," I said. But Juno didn't budge. Then I remembered the command: forward. When we got to the first street crossing, she stopped at the curb. As I had been trained for using my cane, I carefully listened for any sign of traffic then gave the "forward" command. She crossed the street and stopped at the opposite curb. She explained that the dog's job is not to tell me where or when to cross the street but to signal any elevation changes by stopping. It would be my job to find out why the dog stopped. It could be an obstruction blocking the sidewalk that would force the dog to go onto the street, or stairs, or a low branch or obstruction that could hit my head. I had to probe with my right leg first for a change in elevation (the dog is always on the left) then, if none was found, to probe with my right arm to see if an obstruction would hit me on the head or chest, and so on.

I can't begin to tell you how nervous I was. I was terrified of flunking but, above all, of putting us at risk. Although I clearly understood that Emily/Juno would not allow us to get into danger, my mind feared that I did not have my trusted cane, that I was putting my entire safety in the hands of an unknown process. It was like cane training all over again. My heart was pounding wildly, my palms were sweating profusely, and I was having a hard time breathing. Emily finally told me to take a break, calm down, and take a deep breath. She explained that guide dogs were extremely reliable, but we had to work as a team. If I was nervous, the dog would feed off my feelings and become nervous too.

So we started again. We walked a few more steps, then she stopped, and I could feel the handle go up. I asked, "What is going on?" "Oh," Emily replied. "I'm just tired of walking and sat down!" A block later she took off to the side, telling me she wanted to chase a squirrel.

Her aim was to let me know that dogs are not robots. They have flaws, so I would need patience and love to deal with a dog that, even though well trained, still has a mind of its own.

Then I had to cross University Avenue, a major thoroughfare near my home with four lanes plus turning lanes. Nervous? You bet I was! I forgot the forward command, forgot to probe with my foot for the street edge (something you do with your cane if you are a cane user), and, although I was very familiar with that intersection, it took me four light changes to get comfortable enough to "take the dive" into the street.

It is no different for you. When changes, especially difficult changes, present themselves, so many times we get "stuck" in the past and are unwilling to be curious about the alternatives. It is our fear of the unknown, of how the new reality will affect us, that causes us to stick with the status quo. But just as I had to take that first step with a cane into a crazy busy street, or with Emily guiding me, you need to visualize the potential of the new process, your new reality, and take the dive.

No, the transition most certainly will not be easy or smooth. You will make mistakes. The new way may be a step back or may even make things worse. At a time like this, arrogance is not your friend. Are you humble enough to see that you may need help? That you may not have all the answers? That a setback is not forever?

Occasionally you have a happy accident, like when you discover peanut butter cups as the chocolate falls into a peanut butter jar, but these are rare occasions. To bring real change about, you have to be curious, you have to work at it, and you have to be prepared to fail.

Emily and I finally made it home. On the way, she told me the story of Bill, her client who was being vetted for his sixth dog. They were doing the Juno walk in his neighborhood, when his barber, standing at the door of the barbershop, saw the strange sight of his customer holding one end of the harness with Emily at the other end. The barber hollered, "Great improvement, Bill!"

HUMILITY AND CHANGE

You are probably wondering why I focus on the need for humility in a book about change. For starters, we live in a complex world that is getting more and more complex. Human beings are tribal; in most cases, we cannot survive alone. We are interdependent. Our knowledge base comes entirely from the people who went before us. Above all, most of us get huge gratification from knowing we can lend a helping hand.

Think of the guide dog puppy raisers who so selflessly give their hearts to puppies they know will be taken from them within eighteen months. Those volunteers go through the separation anxiety, the accidents, the sicknesses, the destroyed property—and just when the puppies are about perfectly trained, they must give them up. Their reward for all this TLC? Knowing that their beloved puppy has about a 50 percent chance of graduating as a guide dog. It is *much* harder than writing a check for the cost of raising the puppy, and yet these remarkable volunteers do it over and over again.

Then, at their own expense, they come to "graduation" to hand off their beloved puppy in an emotional and tearful moment. And that is the only gratification they get … if you don't count the love they receive from their puppies.

In this case, the puppy raisers are the givers and the blind community the receivers. In my class of six clients who were getting dogs, some of those blind people showed great humility at the wonderful gift of a dog, but others had an air of entitlement. They showed no humility, no gratitude, clinging instead to an attitude of "I know it all."

How do *you* face an offered hand? In Denver, we have a wonderful organization, now called StepDenver, that helps addicted, homeless men get a fresh start. Bob Coté, the founder, a man who literally had to pull himself out of the gutter, had a strict mentality of "Give a hand up, not a handout." He meant let's help people get up on their feet, but not by giving them a handout that reinforces their bad habits.

I needed to learn the difference, to understand that when people offer me a hand up, they are not diminishing me as an individual.

They are offering me a possibility that I would not have been able to achieve on my own.

Pride has its place, but I had to learn that in my transition, I needed to be more humble than proud. In turn, I am now able to help many people transitioning into blindness by sharing my knowledge on available technology and tools. Above all, I can help them understand that blindness is not the end of the world, that we *can* choose the path of light, as long as we are humble enough to accept a hand up.

Think about your situation. What is the change that is so frightening to you? Are you reaching out to colleagues, friends, and professionals and allowing them to help you transition into change? Are you humble enough to understand that there are very few people like Steve Jobs who have a clear vision of their path? That most of us can improve an idea and better shape the future only if we work as a team?

Be curious *and* be humble! The combination will make you a champion of change.

8

Wisdom Versus Imagination

THE HOTEL VIER JAHRESZEITEN IN HAMBURG WAS named one of the top ten hotels in the world in 1975 by *Travel + Leisure* magazine. It was at this hotel that, in 1972, I started my career in hospitality. I began at the bottom, figuratively and physically. My title: pot washer. But thanks to lessons learned early in life, I got myself promoted to dishwasher, then I apprenticed throughout the kitchen as a saucier, entremetier, garde-manger, poissonier, and pâttisier, until I finally was promoted to commis de rang, a very hard-to-pronounce word for … busboy.

I thought I had achieved so much. I was now in the *front of the house*! I got to see firsthand the customers' reactions to the kitchen's creations … got to meet the glitterati who frequented our exclusive dining venue … and got to really polish my "kitchen German."

It was with great trepidation and apprehension that I got up the nerve to approach our god-like maître d'hôtel to tell him, "Sir … I … ahh have been thinking and …"

"HALT!" he yelled. "I pay you to *do*, not to think—so go and *do*!"

In a flash, I saw the two years it took me to get into the dining room go up in smoke, just because I'd had an idea. How many times have we been victims to similar situations, where we think we have something to contribute, only to find out that our imagination is superseded by their so-called wisdom? How many good ideas have died on the vine this way? Are you curious about such imaginative ideas from your children, your significant other, or your employees?

Think back—have you been treated similarly? By your parents, a supervisor, a spouse? Being truly honest, have you treated others this way? Too many times we get so caught up in our daily routine that we resent new ideas. Ideas mean you have to listen, evaluate, and in many cases take a risk. It's much easier to just say "HALT!" and be done. But new ideas are a reflection of your employees' imaginations, not to mention their bravery.

In Germany, being a waiter, especially at a high-end restaurant, is a coveted and dignified position. Being the maître d'hôtel is the culmination of a great career and a lucrative job. So I can imagine how having a young, pushy, immigrant busboy coming forward with an "idea" might have offended his sensitivities. After all, *he* was the maître d'hôtel and I was just the busboy. He might have felt that he was wise, that he was the sum of years spent working his way up the ladder, and that everything was working just fine. But as we discussed in Chapter 4, opening the mind to new ideas can help a business make incremental changes—ideas that might make the institution more competitive, offer better service, save some money, improve the workplace and employee retention, and so on.

No Ideas ... Again

Years later, when I was a student at the School of Hotel Administration at Cornell University, I took a summer job in 1978 as the front office manager of the opening team of the Hotel Internacional Iguazú.

Let me set the stage. The Iguazú Falls are at the point where Paraguay, Argentina, and Brazil share a border. They are set in a pristine subtropical jungle and are a magnificent 276 feet high—a hundred feet taller than our gorgeous Niagara Falls. Brazil "owns" the view, and Argentina "owns" the majority of the 2.5 kilometers of cascades and mini-falls that lead to the main fall, called "Garganta del Diablo" (Devil's Throat).

It is in this exotic setting that the hotel was built. It was the first one to feature elevators, air conditioning, a casino, a nightclub, and modern amenities that were all novelties to the local population who were to become our staff.

The hotel was connected to the rest of the world by a strand of copper wire that had to traverse twenty miles of jungle. The lines were down frequently, so we were often unable to be reached by the outside world to make reservations. This was a big issue as we approached our designated July 1 opening date, a mere eight days before Argentina's Independence Day and the beginning of our winter holiday.

I met with my boss and suggested that we give our head office in Buenos Aires control of our inventory. They could then sell rooms to their heart's content and, when the lines were up, send burst transmissions to our telex machine.

"STOP!" my boss yelled. "You never, ever give up control of your inventory! Don't you see—if Buenos Aires oversells us, what would we do with the extra guests here in middle of the jungle? Hang them on hammocks between the monkeys and the mosquitoes?"

That was the end of the discussion—and the quick death of an imaginative idea. A few days later, I ran into the hotel's general manager. After answering his question about how our bookings were coming along, I shared my idea. He told me to implement it as soon as possible. Which I did.

Then "little Napoleon" (my boss) showed up in my office and proceeded to give me a total dressing down. He was yelling in my face that I was a little punk who had not earned his stirrups. Who did I think I was to go over his head? Grabbing his gray sideburns, he shouted, "THIS is wisdom, until you have these, you never, ever go over my head. YOU ARE FIRED!" He stormed out of my office, slamming the door with great finality.

Here's the moral of the story: when you feel wisdom is on your side, you no longer need to be curious and your imagination is shut down, impeding not only incremental change but possibly all change.

A couple days after that confrontation as I was wrapping up my affairs, my boss sheepishly walked into my office. "Andresito," he said, "the reservations are now pouring in, so the general manager told me to unfire you."

Now walk in my boss's shoes for a moment. I was a self-assured, cocky kid who probably presented my idea with arrogance and might not have thought it through completely, so my boss was naturally put off. As a result, he killed a revenue-generating idea in the bud.

When an idea comes your way, whether from your child, spouse, boss, subordinate, or vendor, are you really listening? Or are you hearing the delivery but missing the message? So often we get on our high horses over *how* things are said instead of *what* is being said.

Opportunities to bring about change do not come to us every day, and some people have to get their courage up before coming to us with their ideas. It is imperative that we create an environment where it is safe to speak up, to challenge the status quo and our current thinking.

At the Vier Jahreszeiten, the maître d'hôtel was running a smooth operation with military precision. The owners of the hotel lived in the hotel and were extremely precise in their expectations and routine. Everything happened in a certain order and with great exactitude. I remember how every morning at six, all the housekeeping staff met in the lobby, removed the Persian rugs, took them outside to be beaten to remove dust, then got on hands and knees with their buckets of soapy water and rinse water, and hand-cleaned the entire marble floor.

Machines existed that would have made that job so much more efficient, but that was the way the owners chose to do it, and it was, after all, their hotel. I have to confess that it was impressive to see the row of impeccably dressed housekeepers lovingly tending to the floor. But as times changed, would the team resent the "show"? Would that time-tested process increase turnover? Would the owners have open enough minds to contemplate the cost savings of a mechanical process?

Faced with so much tradition, the maître d'hôtel had absolutely no incentive to be open-minded to new ideas (more on tradition in Chapter 9).

On the other hand, the hotel at the Iguazú Falls was a nascent business. We had no written procedures, no traditions to safeguard. We had no standard operating procedures, and my idea, however flawed in its original form, had enough merit to be considered. Here, the manager was convinced that his wisdom was superior to my imagination. He felt that experience always trumped new ideas, or even worse, he was afraid he would "lose face" if this young, inexperienced punk came up with better ideas. Do you feel threatened when other people around you come up with good ideas? Do you feel they are trying to usurp your authority? Or trying to take your job?

I have always thought that my job was to get my boss promoted so I could take his or her job. Make the boss look good and encourage my subordinates to do the same for me, so we all grow together. Surround yourself with curious people, and they will push you to be open to purposeful change. And they will make you look great, as long as you are curious yourself and are skilled at separating the wheat from the chaff.

I am sure that you are thinking how time-consuming it would be to listen to all ideas, analyze them, test them, and, if they past the tests, get them approved and implemented. With how busy you are getting through your daily routine, how could you possibly make time for all of the above? And you are right. Ideas will consume your time, and they will require investing your trust capital with your bosses and taking risks. But the alternative is staying stuck—seeing people move past you with promotions, missing growth opportunities, and failing to inject some fun into your life.

Do you feel that the older you get, the more stuck you become in your ways? How many times have you been the one putting down a question as superfluous or dumb? How many times have you been the victim of this? Do you listen with a curious mind to those who love you, work with you, and volunteer with you? We know how frustrating it is when our ideas are written off without ever having been considered. So why do we do it to others?

You obviously cannot explore every idea, but you should not kill every idea that imagination brings to you. Have fun and encourage independent thinking. You will be amazed at how this opens up the door to new wisdom and prosperous change.

9

Take Charge of Incremental and Disruptive Change

JUST AS GOOD IS THE ENEMY OF GREAT, INCREMENTAL is the enemy of disruptive. Imagine you are a successful London taxi driver. Over the years, you installed air conditioning in your car, a better sound system, GPS to better navigate, and leather seats; you took courses in customer service and feel ever so proud of your incremental changes. You are unbeatable. You outperform 95 percent of your competition. Now you are thinking about buying a hybrid car, and you have three techniques planned to get customer feedback and customer contact information. You are cruising.

Then you read in *The Times* that a new app, one you have never heard of, will be implemented in London *next week*. With this app, anybody with a car and a smartphone will be competing with you, stealing market share, working at a much cheaper rate, with less government interference and immediate entry into your industry.

Incremental change is the starting point in making change happen, but understand that by no means am I advocating that incremental change is sufficient. Incremental change only gives you the right to remain in business until you get disrupted. Do adopt a culture of curiosity, of finding different ways of fixing what is not broken, because, trust me, someone out there is getting ready to make you or your business or your job obsolete. Regardless of how much incremental change you implement, that will not protect you from being disrupted, either in your career or in your personal life.

I am not trying to take the wind out of your sails—I am presenting the reality that you *can* have fun in the process of transitioning, of improving, and of staying abreast of—and ahead of—what is happening all around you.

INCREMENTAL CHANGE: A STARTING POINT

In Chapter 7, I talked about my boss who did not want to learn how to type so he could use a computer. He allowed the changing times to catch up with him then leave him behind. Are you being curious about what is happening around you? At your home? In your industry? On your jobsite? That curiosity will not only allow you to stay aware of coming changes, but it also will set you up to become a disruptor. Say that you have set a goal of losing weight. For starters, you need to know your beginning weight, your target weight, and your plan to get there. Your incremental changes, measured by daily weigh-ins, will come from following the plan. Those incremental changes will allow you to achieve the goal. Skip your weigh-ins, skip your exercises, indulge in that tempting dessert, and your plan will fall apart.

However, are there ways you could disrupt the plan and accelerate your progress? Is there a new proven diet or a better way to exercise that will help you achieve that goal faster? Stick to your plan, but constantly be curious about your progress and about ways to improve it.

The first step in bringing change about is to do so incrementally. If, in both your personal life and your professional life, you are not open to revisions and don't have a *process* to explore new ideas, you will be left behind.

STANDARD OPERATING PROCEDURES

In 1980, after graduating from hotel school, my first job was director of quality at the 1,800-room Sheraton New York Hotel & Towers. ITT, the owner of Sheraton at the time, had fully committed to the quality movement sweeping the United States and had mandated that all divisions implement a quality program. I had no idea how to even begin, so the first task I undertook was to find a definition of quality that I could "sell" to employees at all levels of our large hotel.

The one I liked best was: "A product or service that consistently meets a standard." It was easy to explain and easy to remember. But what was a standard? In studying the requirements for the Malcolm Baldrige National Quality Award, the emphasis was on *process*. Every action had to have a documented process that would make it consistent and repeatable.

My first order of business was to establish a standard for *everything* then document the process of how to achieve those standards in a book of standard operating procedures (SOPs). That was a painstaking and arduous undertaking. Once we were well on our way toward creating these comprehensive manuals, I was able to begin the process of achieving the quality standards outlined in the manuals.

Remember Matty and the crispy muffins? She was reacting to the new SOP of ensuring that a muffin or toast be served within the specified amount of time after it popped out of the toaster. Matty and her colleagues saw this as a trivial, unnecessary hindrance to their flow of work. I had to reason with her about why and how it would benefit both her and the hotel. Discussions like that are crucial to getting buy-in from the team. Let them see why the standard is important and how it would benefit them to meet it.

Bringing purposeful change about is difficult and might take many false starts before you get the desired outcome. In my case, it took the entire team working together to establish, fine-tune and, when necessary, change those standards. We had to work together, and we needed to listen to other departments to make sure each new standard made sense and was achievable. For instance, engineering might set a standard that unplugging a toilet within four hours is adequate, but might neglect to include language about leaving the room as clean as it was found. The front desk staff might expect that such an issue should be resolved within thirty minutes, and housekeeping might expect they would not have to re-clean the room after the maintenance was complete. So, the effort took many months of hard work, acrimonious arguments, and even a few resignations and terminations of people who could not, or would not, get with the new quality program. Those were the people who pushed back, who would not listen, the ones who were stubborn and wanted things done in the old, familiar way.

Back to the SOPs. So many times, as I did back then, you think once you have completed the book, you can give a sigh of relief and consider the job done. WRONG! SOPs should be in a constant state of flux. For instance, just as we were finalizing the manual, we computerized the entire hotel, a very difficult transition from an analog world to a digital one. Not only did we have to implement a whole new reality of procedures, but we also had to document and amend them too.

But not all changes are as obvious as computerizing the whole hotel. Some (like your unwatched weight) creep up slowly over time. If you are not vigilant in updating the procedures, employees will see the SOP manual as the "Same Old Process," and it will become more and more stale and ineffective.

How many times have you heard of a friend or relative who was in a relationship, thinking everything was just fine until the day he or she got served with divorce papers? Could curiosity about each other have prevented that "sudden" disruption? Are you asking pointed questions that will help you be on firmer ground with your significant other, your boss, your job? Disruptions can come from anywhere—from a competitor, a health issue, or an accident. You can't prepare for all, or even anticipate most, but a good dose of curiosity might keep you ahead of the curve. If you are in great shape, you might be better prepared to survive a bad diagnosis. If you are the best at performing your job, you might be the one who survives a wave of layoffs. Being curious about what is happening in your child's life could better prepare you for when he or she decides to do something that is his or her way, and not your way. Get the drift?

As an example, do you have a process in place that encourages any team member to remove a page from the SOP manual, copy it, put the original back, then suggest changes to the old standard by writing all over the copied page and submitting it for consideration? You will never be a disruptor if you are not willing to allow incremental change.

INVITING DISRUPTION

Consider Underwood typewriters, Kodak, Ma Bell, and videotape manufacturers. Once vibrant—even leading—companies, they are now footnotes of industry. Did they and so many others do anything wrong? Did they become obsolete because the quality of their typewriters, film, rotary phones, or videotapes had suffered? To the contrary, those companies constantly made incremental changes to improve the reliability and quality of their products. If they were spending a fortune on R&D and coming up with continuous improvements long before "continuous improvement" became a management must, why did they go out of business?

You know the answer. Their business model became obsolete. The manual typewriter companies saw the invention of the portable typewriter. Next, the electric typewriter spaced the letters based on each letter, rather than on a preset distance, a major advance. Then we had the first word-processing machines with their clunky booting-up systems and dot matrix printers. The conventional wisdom was that these machines were too "sloppy" for official correspondence; they were never seen for their full potential. Similarly, Kodak was on the forefront of digital photography but considered it a niche market because professionals would always want the higher definition of film. History is full of great companies and inventions that were sidetracked or obliterated by inventions they should have been pioneering, or at the very least embracing. But we get blinded by our own slogans and marketing, and we fail to "see" the potential of an emerging idea.

The horseless carriage was a case in point, right? Henry Ford has been incorrectly attributed as having said, "If I had asked people what they wanted, they would have replied, 'a faster horse.'" But the point remains valid: Ford's vision was a disruptive one, while others were content with incremental change.

We are now at a similar junction with the so-called self-driving car. The technology is here, manufacturers are spending huge sums on R&D, and legislators are struggling to regulate the unknown. And yet, there are enormous swaths of our economy that are in denial and feel this is far down the road—it is not! The future of the autonomous car, as presented by Rutt Bridges in *Driverless Car Revolution: Buy Mobility, Not Metal*, is truly fascinating but scary. He predicts that we will no longer own the car. Our vehicles are currently idle 95 percent of the time, yet they represent a significant chunk of our income.

His vision, which I fully agree with, is that there will be fleets of cars owned by conglomerates such as Uber or Google that we will summon with our phones when needed. He predicts that taking such a driverless car will cost about a dollar for five miles, significantly cheaper than public transportation. Let's imagine which industries could be massively disrupted if this vision becomes true: public transportation, car and tire dealerships, mechanics, insurance vendors, parking garages, gasoline tax revenue, and more.

Bridges forecasts this disruption will happen within one generation—much faster than the introduction of the automobile, which was thought so ridiculous because of "insurmountable" problems: What roads would they would travel on? How would they gas up? How could they ever become as reliable as the trusted horse?

Think about the ripple effect of this disruption: If you have no car, what will happen with your garage? Or with the parking garage in your building? What will you do with the extra money you will have when you no longer need to pay for and maintain a vehicle?

Far-fetched? Pie in the sky? Maybe. But if you are a taxi driver, an insurance broker, or a car dealer, should you completely ignore this? Are we going to incrementally improve our cars and have the same ownership structure? If I were a young entrepreneur in any of the industries mentioned above, at the very least I would be looking for early exit strategies or ways to join the revolution rather than fight the future.

You can now appreciate why you *must* implement a culture of curiosity and change, as with the SOPs. The status quo is no longer an option. Even if you are doing an outstanding job today, someone out there is planning to outperform you or, even worse, make you obsolete. Ditch the static SOP manual and encourage staff to challenge what you do, how you do it, and even why you do it.

I mentioned earlier the practice of "management by wandering around." Talk to your team members. Work side by side with them, ask them questions, and be curious about them. Talk to your suppliers and your clients, and read up on what is happening in your industry, including every hint of a possible incursion from a different industry. Do you suppose that horse breeders, carriage manufacturers, and saddle makers were curious enough to read the latest press about that newfangled horseless carriage?

I know this can sound scary, especially if you can already see the writing on the wall. But remember: It is all up to you. How you see it, how you listen, how you react, how you choose to move forward (or not) is all up to you. Can you have fun in the process?

How about your personal life? Is it running on SOP? Do you do the same things over and over? Your exercise, your breakfast, your road to work, the peck on the cheek of your loved one?

How do you keep the fire burning in your relationship with your significant other? Are you unpredictable with surprises? Are you inquisitive about his or her ideas? Do you touch each other differently? Do you challenge each other? Are you aware that your partner is learning something new? Maybe working out a little bit more? Changing his or her diet? In other words, are they making incremental changes and are you being left behind? One day, your life may be disrupted by a breakup or by the dreaded "we need to talk," and you will be left wondering why it all happened.

TRADITION AND CHANGE

As an immigrant, I know the value of tradition. It is, after all, tradition that defines us. Whether traditions are tribal, religious, regional, or national, we derive who we are from our traditions.

When I first traveled to America, I met a young woman on the ship, and she invited me to spend Thanksgiving in her home. I had never heard of Thanksgiving. I grew up in Argentina and lived in Germany and France, but I never felt as welcome as I did on that wondrous occasion. I also appreciated the traditions I got to experience in America at my first Jewish Seder, my first American wedding, and inevitably, my first funeral in America. By participating in those and other ceremonies, American traditions became part of who I am.

I believe that we can't feel included in a family, group, society, or company until we *live* their traditions. If you are not a part of those traditions, you are just an outsider looking in—you are an observer, not a true participant.

If tradition is so important, why am I so focused on change? Won't change eventually homogenize us all by demolishing tradition? Will we lose our individuality for the sake of change? Will we lose our souls in the pursuit of change?

When I moved to Miami, Florida, and saw how the Cuban community clung to their traditions, I felt a kindred spirit. I appreciated how they continued their way of life and their religion. But I also saw the downside of their nationalistic pride. They *believed* they would be going back, so they did not need to change and adapt to American ways. They clung to their Spanish radio stations and newspapers, food, and music; they made no effort to adapt to their host country.

I realized that if I wanted to succeed in this country, I would have to change. I would have to perfect my use of English, dress as an American, and yes, adapt to the culture and its local traditions.

I did not have to give up certain traditions I treasured from my upbringing, but I realized I needed to change my behavior if I wanted to succeed. When I was a pot washer in Germany, we had many Turks, Italians, and Spaniards as coworkers. We would speak "kitchen German," but our own mixture of Spanish, Italian, Turkish, and gibberish became the lingua franca. We would hang out together and commiserate about how badly we were being treated. But we made no effort to adopt the German language, to befriend Germans, or to embrace any of their traditions. We felt like outsiders and we behaved like outsiders, making no effort to acclimate ourselves. We proudly hung onto "our ways," not realizing that we were the ones being hurt by our behavior.

I eventually changed my ways. I met and dated a wonderful young German woman, was invited into German homes, and learned to appreciate and participate in their traditions. Did that mean that I was less Argentinean? That I had sold my soul? There is no question I was becoming "more German" and therefore a bit "less Argentinean." For a while, I straddled both worlds, being ostracized by my fellow workers as a sellout, yet not quite being accepted by the Germans. There is no question that I had some serious second thoughts about my curiosity and desire to change.

But I was not alone. Look at the waves of immigrants who have come to the United States. Yes, many created their Chinatowns, Little Italys and Spanish Harlems, but even though it might have taken them a generation or two or three, they have learned to change and adopt American traditions while still hanging onto some of their traditions. Here's the issue: if I had wanted to be purely Argentinean, I should have stayed in Argentina.

Giving up some traditions to pick up others is an important step in adapting to a new culture, whether it is the family you marry into, the company that hires you, or the country you are living in.

When I was managing the Denver Athletic Club, one of the

things we bemoaned was the lack of traditions in the club. Yes, there was a strong squash culture and a strong body of past presidents but, although other private clubs have traditions—political activism, arts, philanthropy, or food and wine—our club lacked strong traditions that would bind it together. The result? The club had the highest member turnover of most private city clubs in the United States.

I do believe you should value traditions, but you also need to be prepared to adapt to a changing world. Clubs often resisted admitting women or people of different national or ethnic backgrounds or religion. We have to remain vigilant that our commitment to tradition does not cause our demise because we fail to see that the world around us is changing. Although private clubs are legally allowed to discriminate, in today's world they cannot survive if they continue to do so. Let us say that you open a club where only white males over the age of 50 may apply. This is perfectly legal, but is it sensible? Can a CEO belong to such a club and exclude his executive vice president, who happens to be of a different race, age, or gender, from meetings at the club? Don't be blinded by traditions that can hurt your business. Don't tie yourself to traditions that are no longer legal or practical or sensible. But be sure to value and guard those traditions that separate you from the rest, that make you special, that differentiate you from the competition. It is a fine line, so be vigilant.

Even the prestigious Augusta National Golf Club bent to current values when they began accepting women and people of different races. They adapted their traditions by finally understanding that a changing world would no longer tolerate their traditional views.

10

Bringing Positive Change to Fruition

INERTIA MEANS THAT YOU'RE STANDING STILL, WAITING for change to come at you, so you are always playing catch-up. In contrast, purposeful change puts you in control. Instead of succumbing to the changes coming at you, it is imperative that you adopt a culture of curiosity, of discovery, of challenging the status quo.

Purposeful change can, of course, be initiated by others, but here we will concentrate on change that *you* make happen. There is casual purposeful change: you decide to wear a different dress, or change the music you are listening to, and so on. But casual change is not worth exploring here. Let us tackle change that is more challenging—how can you bring about major change?

Let's assume you are in a difficult situation with your boss or your life partner. The polar opposite options are to leave the relationship (quit your job, leave your partner) or just grin and bear it, but there are many intermediate steps you could take to change the situation for the better, from appealing to HR to getting a counselor and/or opening up with your partner to air your concerns. Sometimes the simplest answer is the best one, but let's not assume that you have an easy boss who will change just because you share your concerns.

THE MESSAGE AND THE DELIVERY

When I worked as general manager at the largest hotel of my career, the owner of the company was a difficult man. He created monumental turnover among his senior staff and was known throughout the industry for his flares of unpredictable behavior.

One time, he called one of his general managers, told him he was flying over the hotel on the landing approach, and he expected the GM to be out of the hotel by the time he arrived at the property. On another occasion, a general manager was returning from vacation with his family and was met at the airport by the VP of HR, who told him—in front of his family—that he was fired, handed him his final check, and demanded the keys to the company car, leaving him and his stunned family stranded at the airport. The owner's temper tantrums, and stories about his screaming at staff regardless of the setting, were legendary in the hospitality industry.

One time, I was in a sales meeting with my regional VP, the director of sales, sales office manager, and the owner, when my boss challenged the sales office manager on a bet that we were not meeting a company standard. When the sales office manager declined to accept the challenge because "she had a mortgage," he exploded. Yelling at the top of his voice, the owner told her that she had no idea what a mortgage was. He reached into his briefcase and produced a binder that he slammed on the table. He then proceeded to show us, hotel by hotel, the mortgage on each property, adding up to a whopping $1 billion (and this was in 1999). How dare she tell him about mortgages! His message was stated clearly—he was under huge pressure for the hotels to perform—but his delivery made it nearly impossible to discern the message, because you never knew whether or not, at the end of one of his tirades, he would announce that you were fired.

Although this incident was not the most extreme example of his volatility, it illustrates the point. He was not upset that she would not accept his challenge to take on a small bet. He wanted us to understand the enormous pressure he was under to meet his financial obligations, and that is why we should make sure we were meeting or exceeding all the hotel's standards. Many times he would say the right things … the wrong way. When you were under a personal attack from this man, it took a herculean effort to ignore his delivery and dig deep to find the meaningful message.

Without question, the man is a genius. He owns a building company and has designed hotels that work. Aesthetically speaking, they left a lot to be desired, but as far as workflow, I never worked at a better property. He has a clear vision of what he expects from his team and has overseen the building of a chain of twenty-six properties, the largest of which had 1,800 rooms. He created a great company by sheer willpower and the force of his personality. But his lack of trust and his need to be involved in some of the most minute decisions—an approach that worked while the company was growing—worked against him in the end. Once the company achieved a critical mass, the owner could no longer control every decision, but he had paralyzed the team into being unable—or at least unwilling—to think for themselves. The wheels came off, and he lost the company.

Every time my caller ID displayed his name, my stomach would do a back flip, because I had no idea which owner was on the phone—Dr. Jekyll or Mr. Hyde. I had no idea what word that I said would bring about the metamorphosis from Jekyll to Hyde. It was a miserable experience.

On the other hand, I loved my job. We were making great strides, employed more than 1,000 employees, and brought great meetings to fruition. Nancy kept urging me not to not allow my boss to belittle and yell at me. She strongly believed that I should stand up for myself. On the other hand, I knew that, as with any bully, when you stood up to him, he might respect you, but take it a step too far and you would be out the door. After working for him for five years, I was the fifth most senior general manager among the twenty-five properties he owned, as the result of his firing so many GMs on a whim and on the spot. During my five years at one of his hotels, he turned over *seven* general managers, then wondered why the hotel was having such poor performance!

I knew that if he fired me, there would be no golden parachute or anything else to soften the fall. With two children in the upper years of high school, a significant mortgage, and a job I otherwise loved, I felt trapped. We had moved every two years for previous jobs, we loved where we lived, and we had no desire to place our kids in a new school. The owner knew all this well. He told us to target potential managers who were in a situation similar to mine, because they would be less likely to jump ship.

In this case, my situation was "self-inflicted," right? I would not want a "lesser" job, and I did not want to relocate. I knew my parameters. Talking to the owner would be futile. He was an engineer, and he told me more than once that he viewed managers no differently than he viewed a machine part—you maintain it and oil it as necessary, but as soon as it begins to fail, you replace it. I did not want to be replaced.

So I got curious. I started talking with friends and trusted advisors. I read books and explored other opportunities. Over time, I came to realize that whenever I got Mr. Hyde on the phone, or in person, that I had a *choice* about how to react to his temper tantrums. I could make it personal, about me, about my ego, or I could look at the situation academically, listening for the message while overlooking the delivery. I did say that the man is a genius, and many times he was correct about the point he was trying to drive home.

It was extremely hard to swallow my pride and allow him to berate me in front of others or accuse me of stupidity or worse in his insults. But it kept me in a job that I loved. This tactic allowed me to outlast most of my peers and gave me the satisfaction of "firing" my boss when I quit after finding the job that allowed me to preserve my income and stay in town.

To find and even consider this next job, I had to abandon my career as a hotel general manager to become the CEO of an old, traditional city club. I had to open my mind to being responsible for a much smaller organization, one that was in dire need of new direction and excellent management.

It ended up being the best job of my entire career. I made lifelong friends and was challenged at every level to marshal my abilities, not only to maintain the status quo, but also to challenge the team to move onto a path of continuous improvement.

In this chapter, I described two steps I used to bring positive change to fruition. One, I learned to listen to the message instead of the delivery. Two, I allowed myself to imagine a different career, albeit in a similar industry. The impetus for the first step was my need to adapt to a miserable situation with difficult, self-applied parameters. The second step was motivated when the owner announced he was putting my hotel up for sale.

I knew his style, and I was keenly aware that, after the hotel sold, the new owner would bring in his or her own management team. Many owners offer some kind of retention bonus to their management team to help sell the property in its best light. Not this owner. With his purposeful change of placing the property for sale, he forced my purposeful change. I found my new job within a year, but it took him an additional four years to sell the hotel. In those four years, that hotel had five general managers.

I highlight this situation because it is not a "clean" one. I chose for five years to endure a difficult owner, and I took a gamble at leaving my career of choice. I certainly do not advocate remaining in an abusive relationship; I had seen that owner bring senior executives to tears. Do your best to improve the situation or get out. But you need to realize that you are the only one responsible for deciding how much you are willing to take and how much you are willing to give up for change.

BE ACTIVE IN CREATING YOUR POSITIVE CHANGE

To bring about any type of change, whether purposeful or disruptive, you need to be curious about alternatives, about what you can do, and about whose help you can seek. You need to create a vision of the outcome you desire. Don't just go from day to day, taking the abuse and allowing the poison to build up. You will end up feeling miserable, so don't let that happen. If you make a plan and purposefully set a course, you are beginning to make change happen. Will it always work out in your favor? Absolutely not. But you will be gaining the reassurance that *you* are the captain of your destiny and gaining the satisfaction of knowing that you are the one making the moves on the chessboard. You will no longer be simply a spectator of how your life is becoming a wreck. Get curious, explore alternatives, and know that it might take difficult sacrifices to achieve difficult goals.

Change is not something you should fear. Many times we feel that it is best to let sleeping dogs lie. We are too lazy, too scared, or too complacent to take the necessary steps to bring about change. Yes, if you want to change your body shape, or your education level, or the profit level of your company, you will have to work at it. And that work will start with you using your imagination. See the possibilities and imagine the world the way you want it to be. Don't accept the world you are in. Dive in. Get curious. Get the people around you curious. Start imagining and then take action.

Do you remember the ten most powerful two-letter words in the English language from Chapter 2? "If it is to be, it is up to me." Stop worrying about what you *can't* do, the limitations you have, or how well funded the competition is. The Wright brothers were the least-funded group attempting to achieve mechanical flight, yet in spite of that limitation, they succeeded in changing history.

Bring positive change to fruition.

11

Our Support System
Through Change

WE NEED TO BE AWARE THAT CHANGE DOES NOT COME
about in a vacuum. As we know from Newton's third law of motion,
every action has an opposite reaction. Our action to bring purposeful change about will inevitably affect those around us, whether the
change is a good one or a bad one. We also need to be aware of the
"law of unintended consequences."

Going blind is a scary, miserable thing to happen to anyone.
Then losing the security of a job then being diagnosed with cancer
that metastasizes is downright rotten. However, I had the support of
so many friends, the wherewithal to withstand the financial storm,
and even positive articles in the local paper that gave me strength.

But walk a mile in my wife Nancy's shoes. You see the world
around you crumbling. You suddenly become a driver, a caregiver,
and an emotional-support coach. You lose your dream home, and
you move away from longtime friends. You are not in a support
group; you are flying solo into the darkest night.

You have to put up with the mood swings and the new financial realities, just at the time the kids are finishing college and are out of the house for good. How do you handle that kind of change? Where do you find the strength to get up in the morning? To remember not to leave things out of place or risk finding that I'd had a fall. To remember to put everything back in the same exact place or risk having to come and find things for me. To take over the financial responsibilities, and so, so much more.

I am not going to say that things went swimmingly for us. Adapting to the whole new reality of my blindness was, and is still, a struggle, but Nancy hung in there. She encouraged me to do things that scared her, sending me out to ski or to ride a tandem on long multiday tours, knowing that on previous adventures I had hurt myself (broken an arm, torn a rotator cuff, broken a rib, broken a toe, and many other injuries). She was fully aware that if I got hurt, it would create an additional burden on her on top of the financial implications.

Nancy encouraged me to delve into my new public speaking and book writing business, committing to a significant outlay of start-up money with no guarantee of a return. She knew how much I like to entertain, so we entertained. She supported my purchase of equipment that would make my sightless experience as easy as possible.

It takes an individual of unbelievable strength, courage, and deep love to make such a transition in such a graceful way. Change is difficult. Nancy has assured me that she will never get into a car without a steering wheel (we'll have to see how that plays out), and she recoils whenever I update software or introduce a new gizmo. But guess what—Nancy still handles change like a champion.

I want to assure you that, regardless of where you stand on curiosity and change, if you are willing to change your attitude, you will be able to handle even the most difficult of situations. I truly hope you aren't tested, but if you are, I hope you will have the good fortune of being surrounded by great friends and supporters, and you will be humble enough to let them help.

Nancy stood by me, supported me, and pushed me, but there is no question that my decision to make purposeful change in my life has significantly affected her life. Consider how your actions will cause reactions. In the case of my decisions about dealing with that unpredictable Jekyll-and-Hyde hotel owner, for example, I understood that the consequence of challenging him under the wrong circumstance would result in my termination. I chose to bide my time and craft my next step carefully.

The people developing the autonomous car clearly understand that, when they finally succeed, there will be dire consequences for auto-related industries and companies, such as parking garages, mechanics, car dealers, insurance companies, and so forth. Should this stop them from pushing forward? Absolutely not. As we have seen, it is our responsibility to increase our awareness of what is happening around us and anticipate how change will affect our lives.

The cautionary story below illustrates how worrying that we might become a burden to others might result in decision paralysis that could prevent us from getting off the couch and getting on with our new life.

I had just finished doing my first workshop for a downtown Denver company. I decided to enjoy the heat wave we were having in early March and walked to my next appointment at the historic Brown Palace Hotel.

As I slowly came down from my presentation "high," enjoying the wonderful live piano music, a stranger approached me and asked if I would mind talking with her. After exchanging the usual pleasantries, she told me that she had been diagnosed with glaucoma, or hypertension, in her eyes. She was taking six different eye drops to regulate the pressure but had been warned that she would be going blind. She apologized for getting teary-eyed, but she had noticed Pelham, my guide dog, and hoped I would share some thoughts about blindness.

I asked her why she was so afraid of going blind. She shared with me that she was concerned about becoming a burden to her loved ones, then, with fresh tears in her eyes, she wondered how she would cook, move around, or do the things she loves to do.

I went into my "automatic" speech mode and told her that she should not judge her blindness out of ignorance. That she should assess her life situation. How easy or difficult it would be to access public transportation from her current home, what changes she could make to her living environment and lifestyle to prepare for the inevitable. I then told her that her blindness would not be her enemy but that her attitude toward her new lifestyle could indeed be her enemy.

She responded that she was afraid she would not have the strength or the courage to adapt to the new reality. How would she get dressed in the morning? How would she cook? How would she shop?

Still in "auto-speech" mode, I responded that those were all technical glitches that technological gadgetry would help her overcome. That in my Bible study group we had been discussing what humility was and concluded that it meant "having the ability to accept help." I assured her that when I first lost my eyesight, I was a proud man who had to learn humility. I assured her that seeking help was not a sign of weakness but a sign of strength. I urged her, "Allow the people around you to feel good by letting them help you." We talked about the difference between dependency and independence, and how independence was not threatened by realizing there were simply things we could no longer do so we needed a bit of extra help.

For instance, are we embarrassed to ask our children to teach us how to text? Are we ashamed to ask a taller person to put our luggage into the overhead bin? A stronger person to open that stubborn jar? We all have things we excel at, and we all have situations where we don't exactly shine. Yes, the transition of losing skills we have and acquiring a whole new set of skills can and will be tremendously difficult, annoying, and frustrating. Our conversation continued in this way, intermingled with tears and laughter.

When my associate showed up, the stranger and I said our goodbyes and wished each other the best with assurances of keeping each other in our prayers.

After my appointment, on the train ride back home, I thought back to this wonderful woman and suddenly realized that, despite all the "wisdom" I had imparted, I had missed the main point. The woman was wondering whether she would have the strength and perseverance to transition. Despite what she had said, I realized belatedly that it was not about any selfishness. Quite the opposite. Her main concern was not about *herself*, but about her becoming a burden to *others*. I had given her my business card, and I am now praying that she will reach out to me. When we meet again, I want the woman to hear *herself*, not me. She shared with me that she is "fiercely independent," curiously, the identical words Nancy warned me about when we got engaged. The woman's independence and her curiosity about transitioning gave me the assurance that she will have an easier transition than she fears. I only regret that I was unable to give her that assurance in person.

I hear over and over how much people admire my ability to adapt to the new reality. However, in my heart of hearts I truly believe that I am no different from you. When you get tested to the limit, you will be amazed to discover the inner strength that lives inside you. I had no clue. I would never have guessed that I had so much strength in me, and I would guess that you are feeling the same way. Although I sincerely hope you do not need to face such a harsh new reality, I want to assure you that I have now seen inner strength over and over, as I meet people who were forced to face adversity. You have it in you. Be curious about alternatives and be open to solutions, even if they mean you have to make a difficult compromise. Allow your curiosity to lead the way.

Support Is Everywhere

After my application process to Guide Dogs for the Blind in San Rafael, several anxious weeks went by before I finally heard back that I had been approved for a guide dog. They wanted to know if I had a preference for the color of my dog (a question they ask all clients, because some with limited vision prefer to have a dog whose color contrasts with their floor covering). They asked what breed I would prefer (they raise Labradors, golden retrievers, and mixes of the two) and what campus (California or Oregon). I told them I had no preference for a breed or a campus. Then they wanted to know whether I would accept a dog that had been returned from another client; again, I expressed no preference.

A few weeks later, I got the great news—I had been approved for a class beginning July 8. Guide Dogs for the Blind would pay to fly me to San Rafael, put me up for two weeks, and train me with *my* dog during that time. I was ecstatic. It was only one year earlier when we had to put our beloved Rhodesian ridgeback to sleep. Although Nancy and I had decided that we were done with the dog stage of our life, my blindness brought the joy of loving a dog back into our lives.

The next step (yes, yet *another* step) was to schedule a call with the six trainers who would be leading our class. Each of them was in the process of training on campus two dogs to become full-fledged guide dogs. To begin the process of pairing me with a specific dog, they asked many questions about my work, walking habits, transportation modes, general health, dog knowledge, and more.

Finally, I received a package in the mail chock full of audio files to study on dog behavior, dog feeding, dog grooming, commands, ADA laws concerning service animals, and so on. Also in the package was my ticket to California.

I was met at the airport by a local volunteer who drove me to the school, where a staff member and other volunteers welcomed me, gave me a tour, and took me to my room. The next day was all about learning the layout of the facilities, getting to know the instructors, going over some of the theory of guide dog use, and doing some Juno work. (Remember the imaginary dog?) At the same time, the instructors were making a final evaluation to ensure their pairings were correct.

We finally arrived at "dog day." We were instructed to stay in our rooms after breakfast until a knock came at the door. Upon opening it, my instructor introduced me to my dog. The staff sat down with us and gave a full history of the dog, describing the name, breed, color, who had raised him, and any peculiarities. They also gave us a big binder with the dog's full history, vet checks, and papers.

We then had an hour to groom our dog and "bond." Then the real work began: daily walks with two instructors, lots of classroom time, and studying. The days were long and rewarding, and the bond between the dog and client gets to be so strong that part of our instruction was about dealing with jealousy from significant others about the dog-handler relationship.

After two weeks, we were driven to the airport. The dog-client partnership had begun.

Support is everywhere. Many wonderful people volunteer to help match service dogs with their new owners, and many friends and loved ones supported me through the process of meeting my "own" guide dog and ensuring we were a great match.

Even Guide Dogs for the Blind has had to adapt to a changing world. They realized they could accelerate the process of training a dog by giving positive reinforcement and food rewards for per-forming tasks correctly, rather than sending punishing corrections to the collar when a dog did something wrong. After implement-ing this new process, they were able to shorten the training by two weeks. Disruptive change happens, even in the dog world!

12

Change the World to Suit Your Needs

WHEN I WAS THE CEO OF THE DENVER ATHLETIC CLUB, I hired a local facilitator with a great reputation to run our two-day retreat. Board members and I met at the gorgeous new building of the Fritz Knoebel School of Hospitality Management at the University of Denver. One of the key issues the board president and I wanted the facilitator to address was the regular "incursions" of board members into the daily operations of our club.

The first thing the facilitator did was ask us to think about how we drove a car—ideally spending 90 percent of the time looking through the windshield, anticipating changes in terrain, vehicular behavior, road signs, and weather, and any sign of trouble ahead; 7 percent of the time looking in the rearview mirror; and 3 percent of the time paying attention to the dashboard.

Then he challenged us to think about how we ran our businesses and told us that boards and executives tend to spend most of their time analyzing P&L statements, production analyses, sales results, and so forth, all of which are backward-focused or present-focused (looking at the rearview mirror or the dashboard) rather than focused on what was ahead of us (looking through the windshield). If we were looking ahead of us we'd be creating a vision, creating purposeful change, being curious about the competition, understanding industry trends, and researching better practices. In other words, working *in* the business instead of *for* the business.

I can't begin to describe my surprise at the initial, negative reaction board members had to the facilitator's point. The group felt strongly that it was their primary duty to know the numbers and our history, and above all, that it was their *right* and their *responsibility* to give me feedback about our daily operations. It took the facilitator the whole morning session to turn this corner with the group. Yes, you need to keep an eye on the "numbers" (dashboard) and the institutional knowledge (rearview mirror), but to bring change about, to get to your destination, you need to be forward-focused (windshield).

Your organization—and your life—should be lived looking through the windshield. Have a forward focus, prepare a roadmap of where you want to be and what you want to accomplish. Stop spending so much time worrying about difficulties in the past.

When our son, Evan, was having serious difficulties adapting to our local high school and trouble transitioning from the more structured middle school, we used his grades and attitude toward his studies (rearview mirror) to see that there were clear indicators of trouble ahead. But rather than judge Evan for his grades and behavior, we assessed his potential. By looking ahead (through the windshield), and after consulting with experts, we determined that Evan would be better off at a smaller school where he would get more personal attention. The cost of this school was not something we were prepared to face, but in evaluating the pros and cons, we decided to give it a try. Evan's grades shot up and he thrived.

Yes, we had the means to place Evan in a private school, and I realize that many do not have that option. But had we focused just on his grades and punished him to motivate him to improve them, our approach might have backfired and we could have ended up with a disenchanted, disengaged, or even rebellious youth. By understanding the challenge, as indicated by his grades, and by assessing Evan's potential (rather than judging his behavior), we were able to come up with a constructive and effective solution.

Have you ever sat on a board that spends an inordinate amount of time analyzing sales results (income statements), expenses (P&L), and budgets? When I was a board member of the Convention and Visitors Bureau in Louisville, Kentucky, our focus was on how much they had produced, at what cost, who had produced the least, results from sales trips, and revenues from conventions. In other words, we were micromanaging the CEO, so he was required to spend an inordinate amount of time preparing sales charts and reports to satisfy our backward-looking board, instead of spending his time exploring how to attract more conventions to our city.

Give your CEO, your subordinates, even your children a vision, a goal to achieve. Then get out of their way. Yes, monitoring will be important, some coaching and redirection may be necessary, but give them room to operate.

If your dashboard is indicating trouble, handle it. For me, a day without a challenge, a problem, or a screw-up is just another day. It is when we need to handle a crisis that our mettle is truly tested.

Do your best to help bring about productive change that will help shape the future. Challenge yourself to spend a few minutes every day, on your way home from work or on your way to sleep, to ask, "How have I made a difference today?"

The difference can be in your personal or professional life, in the lives of others, or in the organization you volunteer for. Be curious about what is ahead and stop worrying about what was behind. Regardless of how exciting your life has been, always think of how exciting the rest of your life could be.

I mentioned previously the difficult relationship I had with the owner of one of the hotels where I worked. Although I had a protracted "honeymoon" with him, I soon started to realize how difficult, even dangerous, the man was. I chose to learn to work with his quirks and learned to listen to the message and not the delivery. I chose to ignore the abuse and the yelling, in exchange for keeping a job in a hotel I liked in a city I loved, to remain in town so my kids could stay in the same high school and because I loved the community where we lived. But it was a choice, a compromise. I chose to put up with a miserable man in exchange for the life I wanted to have. Nobody forced me to stay at the job. To the contrary, as I mentioned, my wife urged me to confront the man more frequently. In short, I created the world I lived in through the actions, or the lack of actions, that I took.

Similarly, when I went blind, and sudden and massive change came to my life, I had choices. I could live in denial, retreat into a world of self-pity, doubt, and anger, and thereby curse the darkness, or I could light a candle and follow the path of light. Yes, I know, there are many more options and roads I could have taken, but the point is, that I *chose* the path. I had to get curious about the alternatives; I had to learn humility and accept the new reality but not settle down with it. I had to fight, I had to work, and I needed the support and help of government organizations, my work team, my wife, and my friends to create a new reality. I looked forward through the windshield.

What are the changes confronting you? That new boss, or that merger that terrifies you, or a new spouse or child, or a scary diagnosis? None of these changes should determine whether you are happy or not. Happiness is a state of mind, not a condition of the environment. Eskimos can be happy in the coldest of conditions, and a terminally ill patient can be happy with a life well lived. The point is that we *choose* how to feel, we *choose* what fights to fight, and we *choose* when to give in.

Realize that "change is inevitable; personal growth is optional." What do you choose to do? Live in a world created for you by others? Or shape the world to suit your needs?

Clearly, some changes are more significant than others.

I love the old story of the plumber wrapping up at the customer's home. He announces, "That'll be three-hundred dollars cash."

"Three-hundred dollars!" exclaims the homeowner. "I am a brain surgeon, and I can't get three-hundred dollars for ten minutes of work, let alone in cash!"

"I feel your pain," responds the plumber. "It was the same for me when I was a heart surgeon."

For whatever reason, the plumber gave up his career as a heart surgeon to become a plumber. What will you have to give up, or what will you choose to give up? What compromises will you have to make? How many options will you have to explore before you "find the way"?

Some years ago, I took an Uber to go to an appointment. My driver, Hamid, was a pleasant man with an immaculate car. He opened the door for me, graciously greeted my guide dog, and offered me a bottle of water, and we quickly engaged in conversation. I found out that he owns a small limousine company. He has three town cars and a stretch. When Uber came to town, he was angry and worked within his community to do all he could to block their entry into the market. But one day, one of his drivers suggested that Hamid get an Uber account. He thought the idea was ridiculous, and he was incensed that the driver had the gall to suggest it. His wife, though, challenged him to consider the idea. Hamid decided to do it, and as a result, he reported, his business had tripled. Yes, the margins were smaller, but his net income had grown.

He had to get curious and listen to his employee, listen to his wife's input, and be humble enough to give it a try. None of these steps came easily to him, but he had the guts to create the world around him and not be rolled over by a change he could not stop. He looked forward through the windshield.

Regardless of the difficulty of the change, you do have options. The choice is yours. If the doctor tells you that you will die in six months, you have many choices on how to live those final months—fight to find a cure? Check things off your bucket list? Wallow in self-pity and retreat from the world? Be a beacon of light to the people around you? The choice is yours! And yes, you *can* be happy, if you choose to be.

Henry Ford dared imagine a world with cars instead of horses. Your ex-spouse dared imagine a world without you. They shaped the world to suit their needs. Now it is your turn to shape yours.

The shame is that too many times we wait too long. Our boss tells us that we need to change our behavior, there are obvious new competitive stresses in the market, we don't feel as well as we used to. But we hope it will all be temporary, we hunker down, and we continue to do what we always did. Then one day, we find ourselves fired, or our product sidetracked by a new, better product, or our cancer too advanced to do anything about.

Wake up your curiosity! Look through the windshield and face every day with the question, "What can I learn today?" or "How can I make a difference today?" and stay curious.

I love the hospitality industry, and if I had to start my life all over again, I would probably choose it all over again. Losing my job after losing my eyesight was devastating. But thanks to Nancy, friends, and my innate curiosity, I was able to start a new career as a speaker and an author… and I am loving it. You are not defeated until you decide that you are defeated.

The world is not the way it is … it is the way you can make it.

Final Thoughts

CHANGE CAN BE SCARY. OF COURSE, THERE IS "GOOD" change: when we achieve a goal, when someone surprises us with something good, with the birth of a child, and so on. But change is always being thrown at us, leaving us feeling beaten up, bruised, and abused—as with a bad diagnosis, a layoff, a competitor coming up with a better way. It is so easy to feel like the universe is aligning against us. Take me, for example. Losing eyesight in the left eye and being assured that my other eye was "safe." Then losing eyesight in the right eye, too. Losing my job, receiving a cancer diagnosis, moving to a smaller home, the cancer metastasizing—all in the space of six years!

How did I feel? Beaten up, bruised, and abused, of course. When will it all end? Even though I am the fittest I have been in a long time thanks to daily exercise and a fairly healthy diet, I have recently been diagnosed as prediabetic. Now I have to give up sweets, one of my great joys.

What to do? Give up? Get angry? Crawl into a dark space and hope the world forgets about me? TEMPTING! But let's reason this out.

Feeling sorry for myself (which, of course, I did) accomplished nothing except to deepen my darkness. Anger (which is bubbling below the surface) only alienates the very people who are so wonderful at lending me support and encouragement. I needed to learn to be humble, to accept help, to learn that people have huge hearts and have every intention of making things easier, and to let them hold my hand and help me walk through the darkness together.

It is curiosity that helped me get through it all: Learning to use a cane and the technology for the blindness. Looking for a new home closer to public transportation, one that would be easier to navigate and maintain as a blind man. Finding out about great new drugs that have the potential of curing me instead of just prolonging my life. Discovering satisfying alternatives to sweets and carbs that allow me to indulge without risking my health.

Learning to *assess* what the possibilities are, instead of *judging* what I left behind and dwelling on how my life would be better if only I had such-and-such...

See the world for what you can make of it, not for the way that change is "making" you live in it. You shape your life, your department, your company. Our mission in life is to *overcome*, not to *accept*.

Your happiness is not dependent on your job, on your marriage, or on the size of your home. Happiness is a state of mind. Happiness is not something you pursue; it is something you choose to be. So stop allowing outside forces to dictate how you feel. Start realizing that *you* are in charge of your destiny. Be curious, be humble, recognize when pride gets in your way, and practice good communication—asking questions *and* listening—as you let go of your need for control.

Change is part of living. When change comes, it is not the universe aligning against you. You are the master of your destiny, so why not do everything you can to let your curiosity put you on the forefront of change?

Change is scary, but so is going down a zip line or roller coaster. Changing your point of view can be thrilling. For me, a day at work without a problem to anticipate or to solve, a day in which I do not make a difference, is a day not worth remembering. Our goal should be to make *every* day worth remembering. Go ahead! Challenge your team, your family, and yourself to live life to its fullest. Use your intellect, your resilience, and your curiosity to propel yourself and those around you forward. Change the world ... beginning with you.

Guide Dogs for the Blind

I HAVE TOLD YOU QUITE A BIT ABOUT GUIDE DOGS FOR the Blind. I'd like to tell you more. Don't think for a moment that the dogs receive only ten weeks of training! These magnificent animals were born after GDB staff selected which male and female pair would be invited to their facility for a romantic getaway. GDB owns the breeding stock that live in volunteers' homes. When the invitation comes, both dogs are sent to GDB, and once they know they have a viable pregnancy, the dogs go back to their respective homes. When delivery time is near, the dog is brought back to GDB where she delivers under veterinary supervision.

Right away, the selection process begins. GDB determines which one is the alpha dog, which ones get startled by noises such as shopping carts rolling by, and which ones are easily distracted. The selected few are then sent to the homes of fabulous volunteers who belong to a local chapter of Puppy Raiser Clubs. Because the puppies are trained by accompanying their temporary "masters" to school, work, etc., one of their first lessons is learning to sit still. They attend weekly meetings at the puppy raiser club, where they learn specific tasks. They also learn from older puppies that are in advanced training.

After eighteen months or so, the puppy raisers, each one a great hero, willingly give up their beloved puppies to "send them off to college." Each puppy raiser then receives a new puppy and the process begins all over again. There are volunteers who have raised more than twenty puppies. If you are interested in learning how to become a puppy raiser, please visit the excellent Guide Dogs for the Blind website at guidedogs.com.

Puppies that graduated from "high school" with the volunteer puppy raisers are then enrolled in "college" at GDB, where professional trainers work with them for ten more weeks. Then, during the eleventh and twelfth weeks, the puppies' new owners meet their guide dogs and participate in the final professional training sessions.

You might think that the process is extremely onerous and expensive. You're right. The cost of GDB's total expenses, divided by the dogs that graduate, yield a cost per guide dog of about $100,000.

Every step in the selection, training, observation, and pairing cycle has a very specific purpose. The process of pairing a client with a compatible dog cannot be done in a cavalier way; it must be done for the good of the dog *and* the client. Because the process of selecting and training the dogs represents a huge investment, it is important to realize that a guide dog is not the right solution for every visually impaired person. Above all, the GDB staff must be absolutely certain that the dog will not just sit in a home with a client who is unable or unwilling to go out, that the dog will not be placed in an unhealthy environment, and that the client will not put the client-dog team at risk because, for example, of a lack of sufficient cane skills or a misunderstanding about the client's—not the dog's—responsibility to keep the team safe.

I hope that you enjoyed learning a little bit more about the great volunteers and professionals who work so diligently at helping guide dogs help people. It is my sincere hope that you, dear reader, will be inspired to make a donation to this outstanding organization. Please visit the Guide Dogs for the Blind website, or the website of any of the eight other schools, to gain a better understanding of the magical work they do in preparing these remarkable animals to be gifted to the blind community.

Acknowledgments

ALTHOUGH MY FRIENDS URGED ME TO WRITE THIS book, I felt it was yet another thing I had to approach blindly—with no concept of how to write it or what shape it would take. I gave serious thought to hiring a ghostwriter but was persuaded by my friends Jody Stevenson and Dianne Maroney, both of whom are accomplished writers, to let my voice come through.

Writing a book, like anything else in life, is only as hard as you choose to make it. You can choose to curse the darkness of the missing words, or you can light a candle to illuminate concepts that will help others. And yes, *The Curiosity of Change* took an entirely different shape than I had imagined. And no, the words did not exactly come tumbling out—it took me a year to write 32,000 words. But guess what? The book is finished and in your hands!

It is said that change comes about from hardship. In the midst of severe hardship and disruptive change, I learned who my real friends and supporters are. Countless people have guided, cajoled, and pushed me up the mountain, but I want especially to thank Tim Wolf for getting me on a tandem; Tom Dea for constantly being at my side and getting me on the bike through my cancer treatment, and for teaming with me for two—soon to be three—Ride the Rockies; Marcel Pitton for guiding me on skis and for being there when I needed a friend; and Tom Pierce for believing in what this book could potentially be.

Of course, *The Curiosity of Change* would not be a reality without the dedication, support, and encouragement of my wife, Nancy!

About the Author

ANDRÉ VAN HALL, A NATIVE OF ARGENTINA, HAS worked at some of the most highly acclaimed hotels in the world, including the Hotel Vier Jahreszeiten in Hamburg, once recognized as one of the world's top ten hotels; the Ritz in Paris; and the St. Regis in New York. He has managed some of America's largest hotels, including the Hyatt Regency in Atlanta and the Adam's Mark in Denver. Committing to his beloved mile-high city, André was the CEO of the historic Denver Athletic Club for a decade.

A graduate of the School of Hotel Administration at Cornell University, André has served the hospitality industry as director of quality, executive assistant manager, rooms executive, general manager, and CEO. His volunteer activities have included serving on the boards of various Chambers of Commerce, Convention & Visitors Bureaus, Rotary Clubs, United Way, and the Urban League of Metropolitan Denver.

After suddenly losing his eyesight in late 2011, André reinvented himself as a professional speaker and author, focusing on change management and its effect on organizations and individuals.

With the steadily increasing success of his speaking career, audience members kept asking André to write a book that would capture his wisdom and engaging stories about how curiosity can ignite the power of change. He responded with this inspiring book, *The Curiosity of Change: How to Bring Light to the Dark Side of Change.*

To learn more about André or to ask him to motivate your group with a dynamic, interactive, and surprisingly humorous presentation, visit AndrevanHall.com.

Are You Curious About
What Comes Next?

Book André to Speak to Your Team

You are seeing the landscape changing all around you, yet your team is stuck following the same old processes. Incremental changes are implemented, yet you keep falling behind. Your team is dispirited and unengaged.

You are not alone! Our workforce lacks engagement and doesn't care about results. They want to clock the hours and go home. Are **you** curious about alternative outcomes? Do **you** have the power to change things? The power to steer the department, division, or even the whole organization is what keeps **you** engaged!

Would you participate in a sport where you are put on the field but not allowed to use your initiative, your imagination, or your **curiosity** to explore alternative outcomes?

Many organizations are losing ground because they are failing to engage their workforce.

My keynote and workshop on **The Curiosity of Change** will engage your team as we explore the advantages of challenging the status quo. I will give them tools to bring to their hands-on experience, tools that will help *you* implement incremental changes—and possibly disruptive changes—in your operations. I will **instigate curiosity** and inspire your team to be passionate about *outcomes*, not just about getting the day's work done.

Connect with me and The van Hall Company, LLC, so we can explore how to get our vision working for you.

Go to AndrevanHall.com or call 720-339-4831.